THE COMPLETE CHINESE SHAR-PEI

China Chu's Mi Toi So Su Mi, owned by Debbie Houtz of Mi Toi Shar-Pei

Jim Jagdfeld

THE COMPLETE
Chinese Shar-Pei

by Dee Gannon

First Edition

HOWELL
BOOK HOUSE
New York

HOWELL BOOK HOUSE
Macmillan Publishing Company
866 Third Avenue, New York, NY 10022
Collier Macmillan Canada, Inc.

Library of Congress Cataloging-in-Publication Data

Gannon, Dee.
    The complete Chinese Shar-Pei / by Dee Gannon.—1st ed.
      p. 192 cm.
    Summary: Discusses the origin and history of the Chinese Shar-Pei,
an oriental dog breed, with suggestions for breeding, training, showing,
and caring for it.
    ISBN 0-87605-101-8
    1. Chinese Shar-Pei.   (1. Chinese Shar-Pei.   2. Dogs.)
1. Title
SF429.C48G36   1988   88-13291
636.7′2—dc19   CIP   AC

10   9   8   7

Printed in the United States of America

*To Bill Scolnik
and Rick Tomita*

*without whom this book
would never have been written.*

Ch. Bruce Lee's Norman T Foo and seven-and-a-half-week-old puppies. Owned by Debra and John Carr.   *Akin-Fowler Studio*

Contents

Foreword

I AM VERY PLEASED to be writing a foreword for this wonderful new Shar-Pei book. Like Dee Gannon, I have judged this unique breed at many large shows and watched its popularity grow. In my sometime capacity as teacher I have had the pleasure of instructing new Shar-Pei owners in handling techniques, always feeling that my Boxer expertise was particularly useful due to some basic similarities in the two breeds.

I have always been very impressed with Dee Gannon and her work. Not only is she an astute judge, but, even more importantly, she has been at the forefront of the rare breed movement through her conscientious and faithful work with the Hudson Valley Rare Breed Club, which for many years was the only local club offering rare breed events. So she is in the matchless position of being able to produce an unbiased book. She has the credentials to step back and give a much needed overview of the breed and chronicle where it's been and where it's going.

She has done a very careful and thoughtful job and has written what I believe to be the definitive book on the Chinese Shar-Pei. Written for both expert and novice alike, many new details have been unearthed in her history. Dee has also taken on the task of straightening out both the Chinese and American standards. The real bonus of having a non-Shar-Pei breeder/owner as the author is that she has not added her point of view in interpreting the standards but has greatly simplified them for new and seasoned judges alike.

Chinese Shar-Pei have always fascinated me. The very name evokes the oriental mystique. They certainly have had a dramatic history — from an ancient breed that was often eaten by Chinese peasants during times of famine to fighter dog (a sad chapter since this was not their primary purpose, and the stigma still lingers despite their charming temperament now). The breed's dramatic rescue from almost certain extinction to its current popularity stands alone in dogdom. Another intriguing factor about the Shar-Pei is that it just cannot be mistaken for any other breed, despite a variety of colors and types.

The breed is one I would recommend as a great family pet. While some people may feel a certain prestige in owning a Chinese Shar-Pei, I personally hate to see any dog owned just as a status symbol. Dogs, and particularly the Chinese Shar-Pei, have so much more to offer than that.

It is my sincere hope that you will enjoy, as I have, this factual yet delightful book by an author who, as Walter Fletcher said, "knows rare breeds from every angle."

RICHARD TOMITA
PARAMUS, NEW JERSEY

Ch. Bruce Lee's Rumpole De Ruga at 11 weeks of age. Owner/photographer: Alice Lawler

Acknowledgements

IT IS IMPOSSIBLE in so short a space to acknowledge everyone who has shared their knowledge with me. Many have contributed pictures, suggestions and comments to the betterment of this endeavor.

Much thanks is due Alice and Jack Lawler, who repeatedly opened their home and shared their Shar-Pei with me. Alice accepted calls at all hours of the day and night and proofed endless pages of copy.

Thanks are also due Linda Griffin, who took on the job of seemingly endless typing, and to Bob Barber, who went above and beyond the call of duty converting color photographs to black and white.

Photo credit is included in the captions. All illustrations are by Lynn Travers. The cartoons are by Anthony D'Elia.

Matgo Law, of Hong Kong, judged at the first Specialty of the Chinese Shar-Pei Club of America, July 1, 1979, San Juan Capistrano, California. As a result of his efforts the breed came to the attention of many new friends in America.

Introduction

THE CHINESE SHAR-PEI is the most notable success story in the dog world. A mere ten years after the *Guinness Book of World Records* listed them as the "rarest dog in the world," they became the most populous of all the rare breeds.

Over the years, Chinese Shar-Pei have attracted thousands of dog fanciers throughout the United States and abroad. Undoubtedly the breed's rarity drew many of the early owners. However, as numbers increased, the appeal did not lessen. No matter how common the breed ultimately becomes, the Shar-Pei's appearance will always captivate an audience.

Once considered a fad, the Chinese Shar-Pei is now a firmly established segment of the purebred dog world. Their popularity rivals that of the Boxer. Though not yet accepted for registration with the American Kennel Club (AKC), their numbers rank well within the top fifty percent of that organization's published breed statistics.

Today the most often asked question is, "How can you say the Chinese Shar-Pei is a rare breed?" Indeed it would be hard to view a breed with over 20,000 dogs in its registry as rare if the term were applied literally. However, the designation *rare breed* has nothing to do with numbers. It is simply a classification of related breeds, forming an eighth group for show purposes. Where AKC-recognized dogs and rare breeds compete together, there will be eight entries in the Best in Show ring — one each from the seven AKC groups and one from the Rare Breed Group.

The eighth group consists of all breeds not eligible for *full* registration with the AKC. These dogs are purebred, have a breed standard and are registered with a national or international kennel club, but not the American Kennel Club. Note the emphasis on *full* recognition or registration. Breeds accepted into the AKC Miscellaneous Class are still considered rare breeds. Only when they move into one of the seven official groups are they *fully* recognized. Until then the parent club maintains the registry and awards championship titles.

Many Chinese Shar-Pei supporters look forward to AKC recognition. This could happen quickly or take many years. Whatever the outcome, the Chinese Shar-Pei will always be looked upon as a phenomenon that succeeded.

Boawnchein's Bilbo Baggens. Artwork by Jo Ann Redditt.

THE COMPLETE CHINESE SHAR-PEI

Ch. Bruce Lee's Bonnie Brenna won Best of Breed for the third consecutive year at the Tri-State Oriental Breed Dog Club show under distinguished judge Richard Tomita. Bonnie is pictured with her handler, Barbara Solinsky, and owner, Alice Lawler.   *B. Harkins*

1

The Origin and History
of the Chinese Shar-Pei

V ERY LITTLE IS KNOWN about the origins of Chinese dogs, and the Chinese Shar-Pei is no exception. Written documentation is nonexistent. Oral traditions have been lost or are sketchy when available. Most information comes from current research, and speculation and theories abound.

The two main theories claim that the Shar-Pei descended from either the smooth-coated Chow Chow or the ancient Mastiffs. The Chinese Shar-Pei and the Chow Chow did exist in the same period, and these two breeds bear a striking similarity in structure and general appearance. In addition, they are the only two canines known to possess the blue-black tongue pigmentation. Unfortunately, little is known of the origin of the Chow Chow either. The Chow Chow may be one of the basic breeds or may be descended from the Tibetan Mastiff.

The Mastiff Connection, a series of articles by R. G. Harsnell of Hong Kong, traces the possible Mastiff ancestry of the Chinese Shar-Pei. He believes that one or more varieties of Mastiff figure in the makeup of the breed. Breed characteristics, such as the range of coat color and physical makeup, indicate large ancestral stock. It is theorized that the abundant skin developed as the dogs were bred smaller. Further substantiating this theory is the fact that the Orthopedic Foundation for Animals (OFA) classifies the Chinese Shar-Pei as a giant breed because of the breed's rapid growth from puppy to adult.

Whatever their ancestry, it is generally accepted that the Chinese Shar-Pei existed for centuries in the southern provinces of China bordering on the South China Sea. Authorities indicate that the breed dates back at least to the Han Dynasty (202 B.C.-A.D. 220). Tomb dog statues from the period are often cited as evidence. These clay figurines show a short-legged, square-bodied dog with a curled tail and a scowling head. However, Chinese art is highly stylized and the dog was never a favored subject.

Credit as the birthplace of the Chinese Shar-Pei goes to the village of Dah-Let (Tai Leh) near Canton. The Dah-Let Fighting Dog is a likely ancestor of the modern Chinese Shar-Pei. Authorities say that villagers and farmers of the area favored dog fighting as a gambling sport. Other evidence indicates that pirates and sailors used dog fighting as a way to pass time in port.

It is almost certain that the Chinese Shar-Pei or one of the breed's ancestors was a fighting dog. The breed is structurally suited to the "sport," with powerful jaws to hold an opponent. The harsh coat provides an effective guard against personal injury. Another animal would find the stiff Shar-Pei coat uncomfortable to hold in its mouth. The dogs may have been selectively bred for aggression, and some authorities believe that the dogs were given artificial stimulants to improve their fighting performance.

Trade routes were open during the Han Dynasty. The Roman Empire was at its height and the Roman traders possessed many large, powerful dogs that attracted the dog fighting promoters. This lends credence to the theory that the Chinese Shar-Pei's career as a fighting dog was short lived, as the Shar-Pei could not compete against the much greater weight and size of the Molosser (Mastiff-type) breeds.

The Shar-Pei became an all-purpose peasant dog for guarding the home and hunting. The Han Dynasty was a prosperous time for the Chinese peasant. Liu Pong, the dynasty's founder, was of peasant origin and became "King of the Han" in 206 B.C. During the first half of his reign effective measures were taken to rehabilitate the economy, encourage agriculture and aid the peasant population. The country was unified.

It has been substantiated historically that when a nation's people are no longer concerned with day-to-day survival, they turn to other nonessential pursuits. Once famine was conquered, the dog became something other than a source of food. Hunting was popular with the nobility and large packs of dogs were kept for this purpose. The nobility kept mostly hounds, but other dog breeds were prospering throughout the country. The Chinese Shar-Pei would have made an outstanding addition to any pack. The breed is strong and intelligent, equal to any sighthound. A Shar-Pei is physically capable of bringing down and holding almost any size prey.

An example of the Chinese head type. Shongum's Honey Bear, owned by Alicia Kastner.

Dog ownership was at its height during the Han Dynasty, but the ravages of war, famine and disinterest led to a steep decline during the Ming Dynasty (1368-1644). The final blow to Chinese dogs came in the 1940s with the Communist takeover. The Communists considered pets a luxury and imposed heavy taxes on dog ownership. Mao Tse-tung later decreed that pets were symbols of the useless privileged class and ordered a mass extermination. This wholesale slaughter of animals almost caused the extinction of all Chinese dogs, including the Chinese Shar-Pei. By 1950 only a few clusters of Shar-Pei were known to exist. These dogs had been smuggled into the countryside and areas of Hong Kong, Macao and Taiwan. It was a time of "survival of the fittest" and by 1970 only a few Shar-Pei specimens remained.

A rescue operation then began that assured the survival of the Chinese Shar-Pei and led to the breed's legendary ascent to popularity. From 1970 to 1975, a small group of people dedicated to preserving the Chinese Shar-Pei searched for surviving dogs. These specimens were taken to Hong Kong and a program was developed to reconstitute the breed. Among these early pioneers were Mr. C. M. Chung and his protege, Matgo Law.

Though few in number, those early dogs constituted the basis of the Chinese Shar-Pei that exist throughout the world today. As an endangered breed, there were few dogs to choose from and all available bloodlines were used. Early matings involved dogs of diverse type and usually undocumented ancestry. Inbreeding was used to get the breed back to some semblance of the original Shar-Pei type.

The dogs were bred first for type and then for soundness. Once consistency of type was attained, a breed standard was set to guide future breeders toward the ideal.

The type of these early dogs and the first U.S. imports was different from that of today's Shar-Pei. Some of the more conservative Hong Kong breeders believe the large-headed, "meat-mouthed" dogs date only from the 1960s. The historical Chinese type calls for a dog of lighter bone and longer legs, with a "bone mouth" and a horse coat with slight wrinkling only in the head. The preference for the bone mouth in the Chinese type Shar-Pei is consistent with the lighter bone of the dogs. A bone mouth is based upon the actual boney structure of the muzzle with little padding. The meat mouth is more heavily padded with good bone as a base. Lighter boned dogs would be unable to carry the heavier heads.

The term *horse coat* stems from the Chinese horse, which carries a short, bristly coat standing off the body at an 8° angle. The hair is very short and prickly to the touch. It is the shortest Chinese Shar-Pei coat.

Ch. Sui Yeen's Chin Chu is the eleventh champion of the breed in the United States. Owner: Rose Ellen and Morgan Stone.

The more refined look of the early imports can still be seen in contemporary Shar-Pei such as Xanadu Intuition, owned by Helen Armacost.

The Chinese look. Note the longer legs and lighter bone.

The Chinese Shar-Pei in transition: from bone-mouth to meat-mouth.

Ch. Ho Wun Tina. Owned by Ernest and Madeline Albright, Ho Wun Kennels.

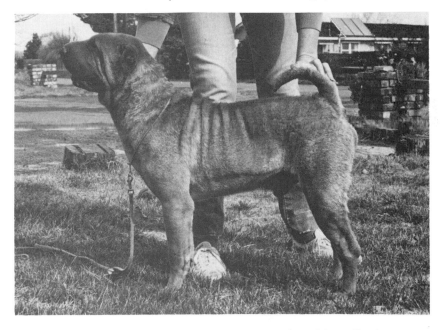

Ch. Albright's Ho Wun II Toro. Owned by Ernest and Madeline Albright, Ho Wun Kennels.

The Shar-Pei's coat is an important breed characteristic and the breed name describes the texture. The most common translation of *Shar-Pei* is "sandy coat" or "sandy dog." Shar is a type of sand that is gritty in texture. This gritty coat texture was desired because it protected the dogs from attack. Some humans may even react to the coat and develop a rash from handling the Shar-Pei.

The Chinese type of Shar-Pei is still preferred in many parts of the world. However, since revitalizing the Shar-Pei involved refining desired characteristics, it isn't surprising that breeders took it one step further and developed a dog whose look they preferred. Today's Chinese Shar-Pei resemble the stylized statues of temple dogs more than the tomb dog figurines.

2

The Chinese Shar-Pei in America

T HE HISTORY OF THE Chinese Shar-Pei in America prior to 1973 is somewhat confused and poorly documented. The information was gleaned from various pedigrees and is incomplete.

It appears that the first Shar-Pei in the United States was Herman Smith's "Lucky." He was bred by Mr. C. M. Chung in 1965 and sent to America in 1966. However, the dog was not registered here until 1970. At that time, the American Dog Breeders Association (ADBA) registered the breed as the "Chinese Fighting Dog." There were five imports between 1966 and 1967. Three of the five were also Hong Kong/Kowloon Kennel Association registered. At least three litters were whelped between 1968 and 1970, and these puppies were registered with the ADBA.

Four names appear in the ADBA listing as owners and/or breeders: Herman Smith, Gwenola Pitt, J. C. Smith and Darwin D. Smith. None of the early specimen were ever registered with the Chinese Shar-Pei Club of America. However, dogs numbered three, four and five do carry the "Smith" prefix.

The Shar-Pei was never promoted in those early days and little interest developed. The first exposure of most Americans to the breed was an article on rare breeds published in *Dogs* magazine in 1971. A Chinese Shar-Pei was pictured, with a caption stating that the dog was possibly the last surviving specimen of the breed. Still no interest arose in reaction to the article. It was not until 1973 when an appeal from Matgo Law appeared in the same publication that the breed made an impact on Americans.

Albright's Ming Yun is the offspring of the first two dogs registered with the Chinese Shar-Pei Club of America. Owned by Madeline and Ernest Albright.

Jayne Langdon

Hong Kong is a British Crown Colony until the end of this century. However, Messrs. Law and Chung feared that it might one day become a part of the Peoples' Republic of China. In order to preserve their work and safeguard the future of the Shar-Pei, they decided to appeal to American dog fanciers.

In an article titled *"Chinese Fighting Dogs"* they outlined their plan to save the Shar-Pei. One paragraph proved especially prophetic.

> Who knows? If we can ship some of our dogs to your country they may some day become as popular as the Pekingese or Chow Chow. We can only hope.

The response was tremendous. They received more than 2,000 inquiries. The demand was impossible to meet. There was a slow trickle of imports from Hong Kong, Macao and Taiwan during the first few years.

These early Shar-Pei varied widely in type and conformation. Many had major faults and genetic problems. The reconstitution of the breed was still in an early phase, and while some new owners were experienced dog breeders, others had no background at all. In addition, speculators saw this as a chance to make money fast. After all, the interest was there and supply fell short of demand. There was still a great deal of work to be done and only a few breeders were equipped to do it correctly.

The biggest problem was a lack of information and documentation. Where most breeds come complete with multigeneration pedigrees that can be researched and studied, the Chinese Shar-Pei had only one "how to" manual — the breed standard. And even that was a relatively recent development.

The standard provided by Matgo Law in 1973 was a product of the combined knowledge of the owners and breeders in the Orient. They had a mental picture of the historically correct Chinese Shar Pei. To this was added the information learned from owning and breeding the dogs. This was the ideal they were working to achieve.

American breeders were at a loss. Dog breeding is more than the mating of two dogs. In the early years a lot of experimentation was conducted. Some breeding programs were well planned and carefully monitored, while other programs were haphazard in order to produce the most dogs in the shortest time possible.

The result was a wide variation in type and conformation. Some say there is a Chinese Shar-Pei for each of the seven AKC groups, from Toy through Working. However, things never became quite that bad. Through hard work there emerged more consistency and lines developed with a certain look. Even though there is still disparity in the breed, you can now look into a show ring and pick out which Shar-Pei came from which kennels.

27

Ch. Albright's Ling Ling, a two-year-old bitch owned by Madeline and Ernest Albright.

Junwongs Camye, owned by Madeline and Ernest Albright.

Among the earliest to respond and receive a Chinese Shar-Pei were Ernest and Madeline Albright. The first dog to arrive at Albright's Ho Wun Kennels was Down-Homes Mui-Chu. She was a three-year-old fawn bitch that arrived in August 1973, followed shortly by an eight-week-old male named Down-Homes China Souel. Both were imports from Matgo Law's kennel in Hong Kong.

Other early importers include Mrs. Victor C. Seas, Lois Alexander, Jean Fine and Renee Lew.

As happens with any group attempting to promote something new, the need for an organization became apparent. No one can hope to do it alone, so the first organizational meeting of the Chinese Shar-Pei Club of America (CSPCA) was held in April 1974 in Vida, Oregon. Attending were Lois E. Alexander, John and Nadine Purcell, Carl Sanders and Ernest Albright. Carl Sanders was appointed acting president.

A second meeting followed in July 1974. Ernest Albright was elected president of the new club. Walter "Dugan" Skinner of Shu Du Kennels became vice president and Albright's daughter Darlene Wright took office as secretary-treasurer. Mrs. Victor Seas was appointed registrar and was asked to establish the breed registry. The possibility of future AKC recognition was one of the topics explored.

Two more meetings followed in 1975 and 1976, at which the same officers were reelected. There was an increase in the number of breeders in attendance, but the going was still slow. The registry was still in the developmental stages. It was not until November 9, 1976 that the first pedigree certificate was issued. The honor went to Down-Homes China Souel. Down-Homes Mui-Chu was the second Shar-Pei registered.

It is interesting to note that of the first 100 Shar-Pei registered, 21 were imports from Matgo Law, 19 were bred by the Albrights, 13 were bred by Mrs. Victor Seas and 10 were bred by Walter Skinner. The 37 remaining dogs were owned by 16 different people with one to four dogs each.

At the fourth club meeting on February 22, 1976 the official breed name was decided and the standard was revised. There were then 30 known owners, but only 19 club members.

An interesting entry in the minutes of that meeting is the setting of minimum prices for puppies and stud fees. The members present decided that the minimum for future *good* pups would be $500 and the cost of stud service would be $200, without pick of the litter. However, it is mentioned that the last five puppies sold in the United States had sold for $1,000 each and three of these were males.

While the club was getting its forms and policies together the individual owners were busy getting their dogs seen. In the early to mid-1970s this was not as easy as it is today for a new breed. The non-AKC-sanctioned clubs were just beginning to allow the rare breeds to exhibit. The first Chinese Shar-Pei shown was Down-Homes Mui-Chu at the Golden Gate Kennel Club Show in December 1973. She and Down-Homes China Souel were shown up and down the West Coast.

The first supported Chinese Shar-Pei entries occurred in 1976. The first Ohio Rare Breeds Dog Show on April 24 and the Pacific Coast Hairless Dog Association Rare Breed and Miscellaneous Dog Match on May 30 were selected. The sole requirement was that there be at least two Shar-Pei entries.

Finally, in 1978 there were enough dogs and interested owners to warrant an annual specialty show. The show was held in Hinckley, Illinois in conjunction with the first annual meeting. Walnut Lane's China Loo, bred and owned by Mrs. Victor Seas, won Best of Breed. Best of Opposite Sex went to Albright's Fawn, bred and owned by Ernest Albright.

Following the meeting a division occurred within the club. Some members felt the original club was too slow in dispensing information and weak organizationally. Another club was formed, but was short lived. The two reunited to form the Chinese Shar-Pei Club of America, Inc. The two registries were combined, which presented some problems as people had dually registered some dogs while waiting the outcome of the split.

Since 1981 the club has grown dramatically. As of April 1987, the voting membership totaled 5,497. On the average they process 30 new applications each week.

The astounding success of the Chinese Shar-Pei in America has assured the future of the breed. There are now owners in all 50 states. American Shar-Pei have been sold to more than 33 foreign countries. The average show entry is currently 60 to 100 dogs, and a national specialty will draw several hundred. Nowhere else has the breed caught on with such strength in such a short time.

Chinese Shar-Pei Club of America, Inc.
Stud Book Registry — Volume I — June 1976 to December 1980

1	Down-Homes China Souel	11	Walnut Lane's China Foo
2	Down-Homes Mui Chu	12	Walnut Lane's China Sea
3	Smith's Ho-Ho	13	Walnut Lane's China Buddha
4	Smith's Swei-Loh	14	Walnut Lane's China Chen Chu
5	Smith's So-So	15	Down-Homes Jade-Ying
6	Down-Homes Kung Fu	16	Down-Homes Ip-Moon-Chee
7	Down-Homes China Love	17	Ausables china Blue
8	Down-Homes China Hope	18	Ausables China Love
9	Down-Homes Ea Ea	19	Shir Du's Shou Ling
10	Down-Homes Ea-Chow-Shui	20	Mem

30

The smaller puppy is Albright's Li Chien Wu. The larger puppy is Beijing. Both dogs are owned by Madeline and Ernest Albright.

Ch. Dor Mon's Titan of Ho Wun II, owned by Madeline and Ernest Albright.

21	Albright's Ming Yun	61	Shir Du Chang Ho
22	Albright's Yang Mao	62	Walnut Lane-s Yu-Fu
23	Albright's Fawn	63	Hong Kong
24	Albright's Shan-Tien-Po Tzu	64	Down-Homes Man Poon
25	Albright's Choo Moo	65	Sue Ling
26	Down-Homes Jade Ming	66	Ming Lee
27	Albright's Ruu Ming	67	Ho Wun II Shamy Ling-Ling
28	Albright's Woo-Ya-Rock	68	Jenny
29	Purcell's Bahk-Jai	69	Dragon Lady's Jade of Gun Club
30	Albright's Ling Hsiu	70	Dragon Lady's Jasper of Gun Club
31	Albright's Ho Hsiung	71	Dragon Lady's Jem of Gun Club
32	Albright's Hsu Jih	72	Dragon lady's Joss of Gun Club
33	Albright's Ying Ying	73	Guy Fung
34	Albright's Neang Neang	74	Chico's Ying
35	Albright's Loo Mang	75	Chico's China
36	Shir Du No Li	76	Chico's Yang
37	Gangis Ka-Hu	77	Down-Homes Ip-Win-Sun
38	Princess-Tor-In Doeto	78	Yu Hui Sheng
39	Ho Wun II Ling Ling	79	Yu Lao Hu
40	Ho Wun II Hsing-Hsing	80	Yu Huang Chin Kou
41	Shir Du Ko Fu	81	Yu Wei Wu Lei
42	Down-Homes Gretel of Eshaf	82	Yu Hei T'ien-e-Jung Yung
43	Down-Homes First of Eshaf	83	33Rds 1st
44	Down-Homes Hoi-Chee of Eshaf	84	Shir Du Lui Li
45	Down-Homes Ningnan of Eshaf	85	Little Mei Ling
46	Down-Homes Ningpo of Starlaxy	86	Walnut Lane's Chi-tzu of Foo
47	Down-Homes Man Sang	87	Walnut Lane's Shih-ping of Foo
48	Shir Du Choo Lang	88	Walnut Lane's Hsueh-Ch'in of Foo
49	Shir Du Koo Hung	89	Walnut Lane's Hsiu-Ch'ou of Foo
50	Shir Du Moo Cho	90	Walnut Lane's Wu-Nu of Foo
51	Down-Homes Man Hing	91	Shir Du Soo-Z
52	Ho Wun II Li Chien Wu	92	Chico's Roro II
53	Ho Wun II Kong	93	Ho Wun II Mr. Chan
54	Down-Homes Ikon	94	Ho Wun II Mei Ling
55	Ro-Geans Loo Mang Jr.	95	Walnut Lane's Ai-Ch'ing
56	Ro-Geans Foo Men Gow	96	Walnut Lane's Ai-Jen of Foo
57	Ro-Geans Mischief of Ming	97	Walnut Lane's Shen Meng of Foo
58	Ro-Geans Ling Ming	98	Walnut Lane's Li-Ming of Foo
59	Shir Due Ling Fu	99	Ho Wun II Lei Kung
60	Shir Du Mei Li	100	Down-Homes Little Pea

3

The Chinese Shar-Pei Club of America

THE CHINESE SHAR-PEI Club of America, Inc. is the primary registry for Shar-Pei in the United States. Since the Shar-Pei is not recognized by the American Kennel Club, the parent club maintains the stud books, registers kennel names, awards conformation and obedience titles and oversees the development of the breed in the United States.

The stated purpose of the club is contained in the Certificate of Incorporation.

A.   To encourage and promote the breeding of pure bred Chinese Chinese Shar-Pei and to do all possible to bring their natural qualities to perfection.

B.   To encourage the organization of independent local Chinese Shar-Pei Specialty Clubs in those localities where there are sufficient fanciers of the breed.

C.   To urge members and breeders to accept the standard of the breed as approved by the Chinese Shar-Pei Club of America as the only standard of excellence by which Chinese Shar-Pei shall be judged.

D.   To do all in its power to protect and advance the interest of the breed and to encourage sportsmanlike competition at dog shows, field trials and obedience trials.

E.   To conduct sanctioned matches and specialty shows, field trials and obedience trials under the rules of the Chinese Shar-Pei Club of America.

F.   Collect, record and preserve the pedigrees of Chinese Shar-Pei, to publish a stud book and registry and to issue certificates of registration.

G.   Stimulate and regulate any and all matters such as may pertain to the history, breeding, exhibition, publicity or improvement of this breed.

Due to the rapid growth of the Shar-Pei breed, the last two goals have been the hardest and most time consuming. The CSPCA is the only rare breed parent club to have its own headquarters building and a full-time registrar and staff handling questions, problems and paperwork. In addition, there are numerous member volunteers who handle other aspects of the club from their homes.

CSPCA Services

The following deals with some of the major aspects of the Chinese Shar-Pei Club of America. Other services are available. For a complete list and fee schedule contact: The Chinese Shar-Pei Club of America, 55 Oak Court, Danville, California 94526.

Directors and Officers

The Chinese Shar-Pei Club of America (CSPCA) is a large, multilevel organization. The club must register, record and monitor activities throughout the United States. This requires a large group of active members.

The Board of Directors is comprised of the president, vice president, secretary, assistant secretary-membership and treasurer. Effective October 1, 1981, nine other persons are elected on a regional basis based upon time zones. Three each are elected from the Eastern, Central and Pacific/Mountain (including Alaska and Hawaii) time zones.

General management of the club's affairs is the responsibility of the Board of Directors. Local club officers are nonvoting members of the Board of Directors. In addition, the registrar, the editor of *The Barker* (the Chinese Shar-Pei Club of America's official publication) and the immediate past president serve as nonvoting directors.

The nonvoting directors receive material distributed to directors, propose subjects for consideration and participate in discussions. This assures the club of maximum information and input from all areas of the country.

34

GEOGRAPHICAL DISTRIBUTION OF CSPCA REGISTERED DOGS
NOVEMBER 9, 1976 TO APRIL 30, 1982

LOCATION	Number of Dogs as of Date (cumulative)				
	1/1/79	1/1/80	1/1/81	1/1/82	5/1/82
Alabama	-	-	1	5	6
Alaska	1	1	2	4	7
Arizona	2	4	6	10	11
Arkansas	-	10	10	22	23
California	47	116	196	346	420
Colorado	-	1	1	9	10
Connecticut	-	1	7	15	17
Delaware	-	-	•	2	3
Florida	5	10	31	71	80
Georgia	6	19	37	52	60
Hawaii	-	-	-	3	4
Idaho	-	-	1	2	2
Illinois	8	24	46	94	110
Indiana	7	17	31	47	54
Iowa	1	4	9	18	27
Kansas	1	11	21	27	31
Kentucky	-	1	2	4	8
Louisiana	-	1	2	4	7
Maine	-	1	3	6	8
Maryland	-	3	4	11	15
Massachusetts	-	3	4	4	4
Michigan	4	16	38	88	103
Minnesota	-	3	7	12	15
Mississippi	-	-	1	2	3
Missouri	4	16	40	69	79
Montana	-	-	3	6	7
Nebraska	-	-	3	5	7
Nevada	-	3	14	18	21
New Hampshire	-	-	-	1	2
New Jersey	-	7	28	77	104
New Mexico	7	9	15	24	27
New York	6	6	12	34	44
North Carolina	23	32	46	56	64
North Dakota	-	2	3	4	4
Ohio	40	74	106	152	167
Oklahoma	-	3	11	22	30
Oregon	3	9	23	42	51
Pennsylvania	10	36	73	114	130
Rhode Island	-	-	2	3	4
South Carolina	-	1	2	4	5
South Dakota	-	3	3	7	7
Tennessee	-	2	14	22	26
Texas	1	10	35	101	134
Utah	-	-	-	2	4
Vermont	-	-	-	-	-
Virginia	3	8	12	30	34
Washington	1	1	9	18	25
West Virginia	-	-	-	1	1
Wisconsin	1	1	5	8	10
Wyoming	-	-	2	5	6
Number of States	21	37	44	49	49
District of Columbia	-	-	1	1	1
Canada	4	10	14	21	32
Foreign Countries	4	9	16	24	33

This table shows the rapid growth of the Chinese Shar-Pei between 1979 and 1982. This growth pattern continues into the present.

35

Membership

Membership in the CSPCA is a privilege and not a right. In order to maintain high standards in the United States, the Chinese Shar-Pei Club of America monitors the activities of the members as well as the dogs.

Membership is open to all persons ten years of age or older who qualify under CSPCA guidelines. Though unrestricted as to residence, the main purpose of the club is to serve as a representative of the breeders in the United States.

Four types of membership are available:

1. *Individual Membership.* Open to persons living in the United States and at least 18 years of age.
2. *Family Membership.* Open to two persons residing in the same household in the United States and at least 18 years of age.
3. *Association Membership.* Open to persons not living in the United States and at least 18 years of age. These members may not vote or hold office.
4. *Junior Membership.* Open to persons living in the United States between the ages of ten and 17 inclusive. They must be sponsored by a parent, grandparent or guardian who is a regular active member of the club. A junior member cannot vote or hold office.

New members must be approved by the Board of Directors. Anyone denied membership has the right to have the application put to a vote by the members present at the annual meeting.

All members enjoy the privileges and obligations of the club. By opting to become a member of the CSPCA, a person agrees to abide by the code of ethics, as follows:

CODE OF ETHICS

As a member of the Chinese Shar-Pei Club of America, Inc.,

I agree to support and be governed by the Articles of Incorporation, By-laws and Rules and Regulations of the Club; and by such rules, regulations, and policies as may be in force from time to time;

I agree to conduct myself so as to bring no reproach or discredit to the Club, nor impair the prestige of the membership therein;

I agree to base all of my dealings on the highest plane of justice, fairness and morality;

I agree to neither buy nor sell Chinese Shar-Pei dogs of which the ownership is questionable;

I agree to conform to the accepted standards of dignified advertising;

I agree when selling a Chinese Shar-Pei dog to fully disclose the characteristics of the dog, its physical condition and to specifically identify any known deficiency when compared to the Standards of the Chinese Shar-Pei in America;

I agree to take immediate steps to correct any error I may make in any transaction;

I agree to fulfill all contracts made by me, either orally or written;

I agree to give aid to members in their quest for knowledge of the breed.

Any breach of the code of ethics is considered "conduct prejudicial to the welfare of the club and cause for action by the Board of Directors." Disciplinary action can go as far as expulsion from the club.

REGISTRATION

Before a rare breed can be considered for recognition by the American Kennel Club, there must be a U.S. parent club maintaining a registry. Once the breed attains full recognition, these books are turned over to the American Kennel Club, so the records must be impeccable.

Since January 1, 1982 only dogs with Chinese Shar-Pei Club of America registered parents were eligible for full registration. With the closing of the stud book to most foreign-born dogs, the work of the registrar has become somewhat easier. The registrar no longer has to evaluate each dog and its pedigree for eligibility under the breed standard and CSPCA guidelines. However, pictures must still be submitted and the registrar determines the color designation.

There is a provision for accepting foreign-born dogs *for breeding purposes only*. Not less than two litters of six puppies after 12 weeks of age are inspected. These litters must be a result of a breeding with a CSPCA registered dog. If the dog and the litters are deemed satisfactory, the puppies will be eligible for regular registration.

The stud book consists of two parts. Part I contains *Plain Numbered* dogs. Once registration is approved, the dog is issued an *R number*. This section begins with R-200 and is still open. A puppy must be individually registered prior to one year of age. Along with basic information identifying the dog, the registration certificate contains a three-generation pedigree certified by the registrar.

One positive aspect of the CSPCA registry is that the breeder may designate a puppy N.B. — *Not for Breeding*. This will appear on the designated dog's registration certificate. Such dogs may not under any circumstances be used in a breeding program.

STUD BOOK REGISTRY -- VOLUME I -- JUNE 1976 TO DECEMBER 1980

ALPHABETICAL LISTING

[Abbreviations: F/Female, M/Male; Colors: Dk/Dark, Lt/Light, Bk/Black, Br/Brown, Ch/Chocolate, Cr/Cream, F/Fawn, R/Red, S/Sable, Sp/Spotted, W/White]

NAME	CSPCA NO.	WHELPED	SEX	COLOR	SIRE	DAM	BREEDER
Absal's Yalgun of Eshaf	270	11/12/78	M	Cr	Down-Homes Man Poon	Eshaf's Quein-Yen	Eshaf Kennels, Cicero, IL
Absal's Youyung of Eshaf	269	10/27/78	F	F	Down-Homes Hoi Chee of Eshaf	Down-Homes First of Eshaf	Eshaf Kennels, Cicero, IL
Ah Choy	R-318	12/10/78	M	LtF			
Ah Chu of Val-Yet	R-402	4/1/79	F	F			
Ah Shun	R-377	5/30/79	F	F	Kwan Chai	Ah Sha	
Albright's Boz	R-373	4/1/79	M	F	Cello of Taipei Kennels	Albright's Ming Yun	E. Albright, Brentwood, CA
Albright's Choo Moo	25	9/27/76	F	F	Down-Homes China Souel	Mem	E. Albright, Brentwood, CA
Albright's Chu-Chu	R-444	2/16/80	M	F	Ho Wun Wun Sun	Ho Wun Tibet	E. Albright, Brentwood, CA
Albright's Fawn	23	9/27/76	F	S	Down-Homes China Souel	Mem	E. Albright, Brentwood, CA
Albright's Ho Hsiung	31	5/31/76	M	F	Albright's Ling Hsiu	Smith's Ho-Ho	E. Albright, Brentwood, CA
Albright's Ho Wun Aby	180	6/10/78	F	F	Chico's Roro II	Mem	E. Albright, Brentwood, CA
Albright's Ho Wun Amy	R-213	6/10/78	F	Bk	Chico's Roro II	Mem	E. Albright, Brentwood, CA
Albright's Ho Wun Bertha	R-202	6/21/78	F	BkW	Albright's Ho Wun Mr. Wong	Albright's Yang Mao	E. Albright, Brentwood, CA
Albright's Ho Wun Bess	184	6/21/78	F	Bk	Albright's Ho Wun Mr. Wong	Albright's Yang Mao	E. Albright, Brentwood, CA
Albright's Ho Wun Beulah	R-227	6/21/78	F	F	Albright's Ho Wun Mr. Wong	Albright's Yang Mao	E. Albright, Brentwood, CA
Albright's Ho Wun CeCe	154	9/17/77	F	Bk	Chico's Roro II	Albright's Yang Mao	E. Albright, Brentwood, CA
Albright's Ho Wun Grunts	135	7/9/77	F	F	Chico's Roro II	Albright's Ming Yun	E. Albright, Brentwood, CA
Albright's Ho Wun Lotus	124	7/9/77	F	F	Chico's Roro II	Albright's Ming Yun	E. Albright, Brentwood, CA
Albright's Ho Wun Me Kong	125	9/17/77	F	FCr	Chico's Roro II	Albright's Yang Mao	E. Albright, Brentwood, CA
Albright's Ho Wun Mr. Wong	123	7/9/77	M	Bk	Chico's Roro II	Albright's Ming Yun	E. Albright, Brentwood, CA
Albright's Ho Wun Quan Yin	181	6/21/78	F	RF	Albright's Ho Wun Mr. Wong	Albright's Yang Mao	E/M Albright, Brentwood, CA
Albright's Ho Wun Sue Ling	198	9/17/77	F	W/Sp	Chico's Roro II	Albright's Yang Mao	E. Albright, Brentwood, CA
Albright's Ho Wun Ting	117	7/9/77	F	Bk	Chico's Roro II	Albright's Ming Yun	E. Albright, Brentwood, CA
Albright's Ho Wun Won-Ton	R-226	6/10/78	M	F	Chico's Roro II	Mem	E. Albright, Brentwood, CA
Albright's Ho Wun Wu-Ti	126	9/17/77	M	Bk	Chico's Roro II	Albright's Yang Mao	E. Albright, Brentwood, CA
Albright's Hsu Jih	32	5/31/76	F	F	Albright's Ling Hsiu	Smith's Ho-Ho	E. Albright, Brentwood, CA
Albright's Kemico	R-556	8/6/80	F	F	Ho Wun II Kong	Ho Wun Shima	E. Albright, Brentwood, CA
Albright's Ling Hsiu	30	12/16/74	M	RF	Down-Homes China Souel	Down-Homes Mui Chu	E. Albright, Brentwood, CA
Albright's Loo Mang	35	5/31/76	M	LtF	Albright's Ling Hsiu	Smith's Ho-Ho	E. Albright, Brentwood, CA
Albright's Mi Chu	R-478	3/29/80	F	F	Tai-Li's Pong	Albright's Ho Wun Beulah	E. Albright, Brentwood, CA
Albright's Ming Yun	21	12/16/74	F	F	Down-Homes China Souel	Down-Homes Mui Chu	E. Albright, Brentwood, CA
Albright's Neang Neang	34	5/31/76	F	F	Albright's Ling Hsiu	Smith's Ho-Ho	E. Albright, Brentwood, CA
Albright's Ruu Ming	27	6/9/76	F	F	Down-Homes China Souel	Albright's Ming Yun	E. Albright, Brentwood, CA
Albright's Shan-Tien-Po Tzu	24	9/27/76	M	F	Down-Homes China Souel	Mem	E. Albright, Brentwood, CA
Albright's Woo-Ya-Rook	28	6/9/76	F	F/Sp	Down-Homes China Souel	Down-Homes Mui Chu	E. Albright, Brentwood, CA
Albright's Yang Mao	22	12/16/74	F	RF	Down-Homes China Souel	Down-Homes Mui Chu	E. Albright, Brentwood, CA
Albright's Ying Ying	33	5/31/76	F	RF	Albright's Ling Hsiu	Smith's Ho-Ho	E. Albright, Brentwood, CA
Ann of Formosa Wakow	R-241	4/29/77	F	F	*Lenlea Ku Yang	Grace of Victory Pet Shop	C.C. Piao, Taipei, Taiwan
Apleichow	R-418	1/18/79	M	F	Joseph	Gigi	Wong Sun, Hong Kong
Apollo of Formosa Wakow	R-416	4/29/78	F	F	Lenlea Ku Yang	Grace of Victory Pet Shop	C.C. Piao, Taipei, Taiwan
Artuk's Ah-Chee of Eshaf	199	5/8/78	F	Bk	Scarsdale's Chairman Mao	Down-Homes Gretel of Eshaf	E. Fahse, Cicero, IL

The Chinese Shar-Pei Club of America publishes stud books designed to help supply breeders with information. A typical page lists the sire and dam as well as the registered color and date whelped. To date there are six volumes available.

CONFORMATION AND OBEDIENCE TITLES

CSPCA rules and regulations governing championship titles follow AKC guidelines, with variations as necessary. However, any titles issued are club titles. Should the breed attain full recognition, owners wishing an AKC title would have to start over. The one major advantage of club titles is that the AKC will often leave the title in a dog's pedigree. Such a designation would appear as "CSPCA Ch." (Chinese Shar-Pei Club of America Champion) or "CSPCA CD" (Chinese Shar-Pei Club of America Companion Dog). This gives recognition to outstanding dogs who may be unable to compete at a later date. It sometimes takes many years for full AKC recognition and often times dogs are deceased or too old to start over.

In order to earn points toward a championship title or legs toward an obedience title, the dog must be individually registered and the owner must be a member of the club. Dogs may be shown under their litter number for only 30 days following their first show unless an extension is granted.

Points and legs are earned at *sanctioned* CSPCA shows, which means that the event has been approved by the CSPCA prior to the show date. To receive sanctioning, a sponsoring club must submit the required forms and fees and comply with CSPCA regulations. This applies to both affiliated and nonaffiliated clubs sponsoring Chinese Shar-Pei shows. Listings of sanctioned shows are available from the CSPCA.

To date, judges are not individually licensed or sanctioned. However, judges' names must be listed on the sanctioning form and are subject to CSPCA approval.

Championship points are awarded under the following schedule:

Points	Dogs	Bitches
1	2	2
2	3	3
3	6	6
4	9	9
5	15	15

The point system is subject to change, but the most recent schedule can be obtained by writing the CSPCA.

Further booklets, such as "Rules Applying to Registration and Dog shows" and "Obedience Regulations," are available free of charge from the American Kennel Club, 51 Madison Avenue, New York, NY 10010. Individual owners are currently responsible for obtaining the information and signatures required to validate wins.

SPECIALTY SHOWS

Specialties for Chinese Shar-Pei can only be sponsored by CSPCA-affiliated clubs. The rules governing specialties are available from the CSPCA.

The major difference between affiliated specialty shows and nonaffiliated sanctioned shows is the judging requirements. The judge of a specialty must be AKC licensed, while at all other shows there is no such requirement.

Affiliated clubs are limited to two specialties per year and they must be at least four months apart.

SANCTIONED SHOWS

Sanctioned events are CSPCA approved shows. Sanctioning is available to affiliated and nonaffiliated clubs.

Affiliated clubs are limited to two sanctioned shows each year and they must be four months apart. Sanctioned shows are not specialties. Other breeds may be invited to exhibit. Only an affiliated club can sponsor a two-day weekend show. One show would be sanctioned and the other show would be a specialty. Each affiliated club may hold four shows each year — two sanctioned shows and two specialties.

Nonaffiliated clubs are limited to four sanctioned shows each year and each show must be at least two months apart. There are no provisions for a nonaffiliated club to host a two-day weekend show. Two separate clubs must sponsor the Chinese Shar-Pei entry, if both shows are held in one weekend.

The Barker

The Barker is the official publication of the CSPCA. The magazine is published bimonthly and contains information on all Chinese Shar-Pei activities throughout the United States. There are reports from the board, lists of new member applications, articles, breeder lists, information on new champions and obedience titlists, show results, litter information, general editorials and advertisements. Advertising is limited to the membership.

REGISTERING ORGANIZATIONS

American Dog Breeders Association

Before the CSPCA was even thought of, the American Dog Breeders Association (ADBA) accepted the Shar-Pei for registration as the Chinese

Fighting Dog. They registered their first dog in 1970. The breed is no longer registered with this organization.

United Kennel Club, Inc.

In 1985 the United Kennel Club (UKC) made a unilateral decision to open their registry to the Chinese Shar-Pei. The UKC is the second largest registry in the United States (the AKC is the largest).

After extended negotiations with the CSPCA, the UKC recognized the breed — against the wishes of the parent club. Initially, the CSPCA had rules disciplining anyone registering their Shar-Pei with the UKC. However, it was determined that this would be restraint of trade and the rules were revoked.

The CSPCA does not endorse registration with the UKC, but recognizes that some owners may do so for obedience purposes. With little interest in UKC registration by the CSPCA members, no conformation shows or judges have been licensed by that organization.

The goal of the majority of the CSPCA members is AKC recognition.

Hong Kong and Kowloon Kennel Association

Many early Shar-Pei were registered with the Hong Kong and Kowloon Kennel Association (HKKA). This association still maintains stud books and registers foreign-born dogs.

The HKKA should not be confused with the Hong Kong Kennel Club (HKKC), which does not keep a separate registry for the Chinese Shar-Pei. The HKKC discontinued registering the breed in 1966, the reported reason being that the dogs applying for registration no longer had the appearance or type of the dogs formerly registered. The more recent dogs had muzzles that were more flashy, the head and body were excessively wrinkled and the coat was longer and/or softer. There was some suspicion that these modifications had resulted from crossbreedings.

Taiwan Kennel Club

An affiliate of the Asian Kennel Union (AKU), the Taiwan Kennel Club (TKC) continues to register foreign Chinese Shar-Pei.

Federation Cynologique Internationale

The Chinese Shar-Pei has been accepted by the distinguished international organization, the Federation Cynologique Internationale (FCI). This means the breed is eligible for recognition in FCI affiliated countries and may be shown at international shows for certificates toward titles.

Various other countries are in the process of recognizing the Shar-Pei, but the breed is still too new to have become firmly established in most areas. The United States remains the largest and most organized of the Chinese Shar-Pei populated areas.

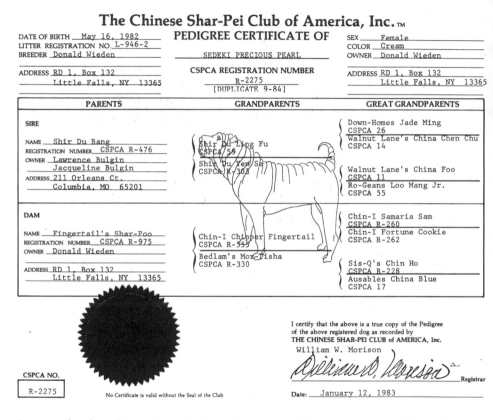

The Chinese Shar-Pei Club of America, Inc. ™

DATE OF BIRTH __May 16, 1982__
LITTER REGISTRATION NO. __L-946-2__
BREEDER __Donald Wieden__

ADDRESS __RD 1, Box 132__
__Little Falls, NY 13365__

PEDIGREE CERTIFICATE OF

__SEDEKI PRECIOUS PEARL__

CSPCA REGISTRATION NUMBER
__R-2275__
[DUPLICATE 9-84]

SEX __Female__
COLOR __Cream__
OWNER __Donald Wieden__

ADDRESS __RD 1, Box 132__
__Little Falls, NY 13365__

PARENTS	GRANDPARENTS	GREAT GRANDPARENTS
SIRE NAME __Shir Du Bang__ REGISTRATION NUMBER __CSPCA R-476__ OWNER __Lawrence Bulgin__ __Jacqueline Bulgin__ ADDRESS __211 Orleans Ct.__ __Columbia, MO 65201__	Shir Du Ling Fu CSPCA 59 Shir Du Yen Se CSPCA R-303	Down-Homes Jade Ming CSPCA 26 Walnut Lane's China Chen Chu CSPCA 14 Walnut Lane's China Foo CSPCA 11 Ro-Geans Loo Mang Jr. CSPCA 55
DAM NAME __Fingertail's Shar-Poo__ REGISTRATION NUMBER __CSPCA R-975__ OWNER __Donald Wieden__ ADDRESS __RD 1, Box 132__ __Little Falls, NY 13365__	Chin-I Chipper Fingertail CSPCA R-555 Bedlam's Mor-Tisha CSPCA R-330	Chin-I Samaria Sam CSPCA R-260 Chin-I Fortune Cookie CSPCA R-262 Sis-Q's Chin Ho CSPCA R-228 Ausables China Blue CSPCA 17

CSPCA NO.

R-2275

No Certificate is valid without the Seal of the Club

I certify that the above is a true copy of the Pedigree of the above registered dog as recorded by
THE CHINESE SHAR-PEI CLUB of AMERICA, Inc.
William W. Morison

_____ Registrar

Date: __January 12, 1983__

An example of a Chinese Shar-Pei Club of America official registration certificate. Each certificate contains a three-generation pedigree.

4

The Chinese Shar-Pei Standard

THE FIRST AND ONLY "how to" manual for early Chinese Shar-Pei breeders in America was the Hong Kong and Kowloon Kennel Association (HKKA) standard.

The standard is a written description of the ideal Chinese Shar-Pei. Each part of the dog is defined and described, with both good and bad points discussed. A Shar-Pei that conforms closely to the written standard is correct. Though there are no perfect dogs, some come closer to the ideal than others. The challenge and art of breeding are to move closer and closer with each mating to that perfect specimen.

To date there have been four standards for the Chinese Shar-Pei in the United States. The HKKA standard was developed by Matgo Law and other knowledgeable breeders in the Orient at the request of the American owners. The resulting standard stressed the Shar-Pei's unique characteristics, described the goals of Hong Kong breeders and provided a guideline for those in other countries.

PROVISIONAL STANDARD OF CHINESE SHAR-PEI
(Hong Kong and Kowloon Kennel Association)

ORIGIN AND CHARACTERISTICS. This is a real Chinese breed existing for centuries in the southern provinces near the south China Sea. The original fountain is believed in a town, "Dah Let" in Kwun Tung Province. Dogfighting was the pastime of the farmers and small town dwellers since other entertainment was scarcely available then. The breed is equipped with all the features of a gladiator, which will be mentioned by points in the following structural descriptions. The very particular feature is the bluish-black tongue as the Chow Chow. With the addition

Ch. Bruce Lee's Kai Tug Lee, owned by Elly Paulus.

of the similar dignified expression and excellent guarding instinct, it is believed that both the breeds were from the same origin. However, the Chinese Fighting Dog, as the breed was formerly known, is by no means a smooth-coated Chow. They may come from the same fountainhead or perhaps the former is descended from the latter.

In character, he is not a born fighter, but loves to do so, should the owner provoke since young. Instead, he is a well-balanced dog with a dignified scowling expression; loyal, yet aloof, reserved to strangers while devoted to his family. He needs not to be trained; a natural excellent household guard and self-housebroken.

GENERAL APPEARANCE. An active, compact, short-coupled dog, well knit in frame, giving a square build, standing firm on ground with the calm and firm stature of a severe warrior.

HEAD AND SKULL. Skull flat and broad, rather large in proportion with the body, with little stop. Profuse and fine wrinkles appear upon the forehead and cheek, and continue to form the heavy dewlaps. Muzzle moderately long and broad from the eyes to the point of nose (without any suggestion of tapering but rather in the mouth-shape of a hippopotamus).

NOSE. Black, large and wide, occasionally there are cream dogs with brick-colored nose and light fawn dogs with self-colored nose, but black is preferable.

EYES. Dark, small, almond shaped and sunken (light color is found in cream and light fawn dogs). The sunken small eyes are advantageous in dog-fighting to reduce chances of injury to the eyes. Also, the sunken eyes and wrinkles upon the forehead help the scowling expression of the breed.

MOUTH. Teeth strong and level, giving scissors bite, the canines are somewhat curved (increasing the difficulty of freeing the grip). Tongue bluish-black. Flews and roof of mouth black. Gums preferably black.

EARS. Small, rather thick, equilateral triangular in shape and slightly rounded at the tip, set well forward over the eyes and wide apart. In contrast to the Chow Chow the ears should set as tightly to the skull and as small as possible. It minimizes the opportunity of his opponent to get a grip on the ears. Some specimen have ears so small as the size of a human thumb nail, just covering the ear burr.

NECK. Strong, full, set well on the shoulders with heavy folding skin and abundant dewlaps.

FOREQUARTERS. Shoulders muscular and sloping. Forelegs straight, of moderate length with good bone.

BODY. Chest broad and deep, back short; topline, slightly dipped behind the withers, rises to meet the root of the tail, which is set high on the loin.

Echoing the wrinkles and dewlaps, there is a lot of skin folding on the body. The abundant loose skin allows spaces for the warrior to turn and attack even though a certain part of the body is gripped by his opponent.

HINDQUARTERS. Hindlegs muscular and strong, hocks slightly bent and well let down, giving length and strength from loins to hock. (Not so straight as the Chow.)

FEET. Moderate in size, compact and firmly set, toes well split up, with high knuckles; giving firm stand.

TAIL. Thick and round at the base, then evenly tapering to a fine point. The three ways of carriage are described as follows, in order of merit: The most desirable is the type set on top and curled over to either side — some curled so tightly as to present the shape of a small ringlet, only in the size of a large ancient China coin. The second type is curled in a loose ring. The third type is carried high in a curve toward the back, not touching the back. This carriage allows the dog to wiggle in a happier and more eager fashion. On either type, the tail should be set high on the loin, showing the anus.

COAT. Another peculiar feature of the breed. The coat is extremely short (shorter than the Bulldogs' and a similar coat is considered as to be too long) and bristly, and unusually harsh to touch. It is a coat absolutely uncomfortable to be held in any canine mouth. It is not lustrous as the coat of a Doberman but by no means gives the impression of an unhealthy coat.

COLOUR. Whole colours — black, red, deep fawn, light fawn and cream, frequently shaded (the underpart of tail and back of thighs of a lighter colour but not in patches or parti-coloured).

WEIGHT AND SIZE. Around 18-20 inches at withers; weight 40-50 lbs. Dog is heavier than bitch and more squarely built. The balance of an individual is important.

FAULTS. Spotted tongue. Tail carried horizontally or covering the anus. A flat, long, shining coat (the coat is not harsh and off-standing). Tapering muzzle like a fox (not blunt enough).

THE AMERICAN STANDARD

Early Chinese Shar-Pei varied in type and conformation. Very few met the HKKA standard. However, remember that the HKKA standard was a projection of the ideal Shar-Pei once the breed was reestablished and refined.

The members of the original Chinese Shar-Pei Club of America decided a more generalized standard was necessary. This standard would encompass the varying types currently in the United States. It was stated that later the standard could be revised and refined as the American Shar-Pei became more consistent.

A 32 statement standard was drafted and sent to the 30 known Shar-Pei owners for review. Only 15 signatures were required for approval.

A letter was sent with the standard stating: "Each owner must adopt, reject or modify each sentence of the general description, based on characteristics of their own Shar-Pei, photos or features they have seen of other Shar-Peis and other Shar-Pei knowledge they have."

Here the Hong Kong breeders and the American breeders parted ways.

46

A gaggle of puppies owned by Elly Paulus.

Xanadu Intuition at
three months of age.
Owner: Helen
Armacost.

47

Ch. Oriental Treasure's Put N On The Ritz on the left, owned by Maryann Smithers, and Ch. Noahs Ark Blackberry, CD, on the right, owned by Helen Armacost.

Ch. Chow Wen Go Kaboom on the left and a Wrinky daughter on the right. Both are owned by Linda and Mike Schatzberg. *Crezentia Allen*

Each group was breeding toward a different ideal. This is why some conservative Hong Kong breeders say the American Shar-Pei is different from the historical Chinese Shar-Pei. The heavier head, greater abundance of wrinkles, longer coats and heavier bodies were not part of the original plan.

During the breakup of the original CSPCA into two clubs yet another standard was developed. That standard made further allowances.

Finally, the two clubs reunited and on January 1, 1982 a revised standard was adopted. It tightened the breed description and specified faults. This standard came closer to the HKKA standard, with variations accommodating some, but not all of the characteristics of American Shar-Pei.

Any and all references to fighting dogs and the Chow Chow were removed. Although the height specifications remained the same, the average weight range was broadened five pounds in both directions. This provision allowed for heavier, more muscular dogs than the original imports.

The description of the muzzle was expanded and the first reference to padding appeared. The addition of light purple and spotted or flowered mouths as an acceptable breed feature was a major deviation from the original standard.

The tail description was generalized in the new standard. The original standard called for three specific tail carriages; the new standard only stated that the tail should curl over the back. Also, a misleading sentence was added. The new standard stated, "No tail is a major fault." To someone experienced with standards, the sentence means the absence of a tail is a major fault. However, not everyone interpreted it this way. The other, more literal interpretation was that tails were not to be majorly faulted. This resulted in several bob-tailed dogs placing well at conformation shows.

The coat and color descriptions were also generalized. The "extremely short" coat became "a coat over one inch is a major fault." No reference was made to the unusual harshness or the texture. Also, the standard stated that the coat "appears healthy, without being shiny or lustrous." The original standard referred to the coat of the Doberman when describing luster. There is a difference between the shine of a healthy Shar-Pei coat and the luster of a Doberman coat.

The writers of the new standard chose not to specify any coat colors. Any color was allowed as long as it was a whole color. The definition of each coat color accepted in the registry was written as a separate set of descriptions.

The addition to the standard of a description of proper gait was a definite plus. Many judges consider movement as important as overall conformation. If a dog is not structured properly, it cannot move well. However, each breed has a distinctive movement that needs to be defined.

This standard took effect on October 1, 1982 and was used until January 1, 1985, when another revised standard took effect.

OFFICIAL CHINESE SHAR-PEI STANDARD
Chinese Shar-Pei Club of America, Inc.

GENERAL APPEARANCE. An active, compact dog of medium size and substance, square in profile, close coupled, the head somewhat large for the body. The short harsh coat, the loose skin covering the head and the body and the typical muzzle shape imparts to the Shar-Pei a unique individual stamp peculiar to him alone. The loose skin and wrinkles are superabundant in puppies but these features are less exaggerated in the adult.

HEAD. Large, proudly carried and covered with profuse and fine wrinkles on the forehead and cheek.

Skull — Flat and broad the stop moderately defined, the length from nose to stop is approximately the same as from stop to occiput. *Muzzle* — One of the distinctive features of the breed. It is broad and full with no suggestion of snipiness. The lips and top of muzzle are well padded, causing a slight bulge at the base of the nose. When viewed from the front, the bottom jaw appears to be wider than the top jaw due to the excessive padding of the lips. *Nose* — large and wide and darkly pigmented, preferably black, but any color conforming to the general coat color of the dog is acceptable. *Teeth* — Strong, meeting in a scissors bite, the canines somewhat curved. *Eyes* — Dark, extremely small, almond shaped and sunken, displaying a scowling expression. A somewhat lighter eye is acceptable in lighter colored dogs. *Ears* — Extremely small, rather thick, equilateral triangles in shape, slightly rounded at the tips. They lie flat against the head and are set wide apart and forward on the skull with the tips pointing toward the eyes. The ears are not without erectile power but a prick ear is a major fault. *Tongue, Roof of Mouth, Gums and Flews* — Solid bluish-black is preferred. Light purple or spotted (flowered) mouths are acceptable. A solid pink tongue is a major fault.

BODY. *Neck* — Medium length, strong, full and set well into the shoulders. There are heavy folds of loose skin and abundant dewlap about the neck and throat. *Back* — Short and close coupled, the topline dips slightly behind the withers, slightly rising over the short, broad loin. *Chest* — Broad and deep with the brisket extending to the elbow and rising slightly under the loin. *Croup* — Slightly sloping with the base of the tail set extremely high, clearly exposing a protruding anus. *Tail* — Thick and round at the base, tapering to a fine point and curling over the back. No tail is a major fault.

FOREQUARTERS. *Shoulders* — Muscular, well laid back and sloping. *Forelegs* — When viewed from the front, straight, moderately spaced with elbows close to the body. When viewed from the side, the forelegs are staight, the pasterns sightly bent, strong and flexible. The bone is substantial but never heavy and is of

50

moderate length. *Feet* — Moderate in size, compact, well knuckled up and firmly set. *Dewclaws* — Removal of front dewclaws is optional.

HINDQUARTERS. Muscular, strong and moderately angulated, the hock well let down. *Dewclaws* — Hind dewclaws should be removed.

COAT. The extremely harsh coat is one of the distinguishing features of the breed. The coat is absolutely straight and offstanding on the main trunk of the body but generally lies somewhat flatter on the limbs; there is no undercoat. The coat appears healthy, without being shiny or lustrous. A coat over one inch is a major fault. The Shar-Pei is shown in as natural a state as is consistent with good grooming. The coat must not be trimmed in any way. A coat that has been trimmed is to be severely penalized.

COLOR. Solid colors. A solid-colored dog may have shading but not in patches or spots. A dog that is patched or spotted is a major fault.

GAIT. Free and balanced with the rear feet tending to converge on a center line of gravity when the dog moves at a vigorous trot.

SIZE. Average height is 18 to 20 inches at the withers. Average weight is 35 to 55 pounds. The dog is usually larger and more square bodied than the bitch, but in either case should appear well proportioned.

TEMPERAMENT. Alert, dignified, lordly, scowling, discerning, sober and snobbish, essentially independent and somewhat standoffish but extreme in his devotion.

The most recent standard has further tightened the description of the ideal Chinese Shar-Pei. It was revised April 1, 1987 and voted in at the annual meeting in May 1987, with provision that some wording be changed or modified. The final draft of the standard was made on July 18, 1987, taking effect January 1, 1988.

The Board of Directors believe the American Chinese Shar-Pei has stabilized to the point that disqualifying faults are needed to weed out the inferior dogs.

Many questionable points that judges have raised over the years have been stated in terms everyone can understand.

STANDARD OF THE CHINESE SHAR-PEI IN AMERICA
(Effective January 1, 1988)
Chinese Shar-Pei Club of America, Inc.

GENERAL APPEARANCE. An alert, dignified, active, compact dog of medium size and substance, square in profile, close-coupled, the well-proportioned head slightly but not overly large for the body. The short, harsh coat; the loose skin covering the head and body; the small ears; the "hippopotamus" muzzle shape and the high-set tail impart to the Shar-Pei a unique look peculiar to him alone. The loose skin and wrinkles covering the head, neck and body are superabundant in puppies but these features may be limited to the head, neck and withers in the adult.

HEAD. Large, slightly but not overly, proudly carried and covered with profuse wrinkles on the forehead continuing into side wrinkles framing the face. *Skull* — Flat and broad, the stop moderately defined, the length from nose to stop is approximatley the same as from stop to occiput. *Muzzle* — One of the distinctive features of the breed. It is broad and full with no suggestion of snipiness. The lips and top of muzzle are well padded and may cause a slight bulge at the base of the nose. *Nose* — Large and wide and darkly pigmented, preferably black but any color nose conforming to the general coat color of the dog is acceptable. In dilute colors, the preferred nose is self-colored. Darkly pigmented cream Shar-Pei may have some light pigment either in the center of their noses or on their entire nose. *Teeth* — Strong, meeting in a scissors bite. Deviation from scissors bite is a major fault. *Eyes* — Dark, small, almond-shaped and sunken, displaying a scowling expression. In the dilute colored dogs the eye color may be lighter. *Ears* — Extremely small, rather thick, equilateral triangles in shape, slightly rounded at the tips, edges of the ear may curl. Ears lie flat against the head, are set wide apart and forward on the skull, pointing toward the eyes. The ears have the ability to move. Pricked ears are a disqualification. *Tongue,, Roof of Mouth, Gums and Flews* — Solid bluish-black is preferred in all coat colors except in dilute colors, which have a solid lavender pigmentation. A spotted tongue is a major fault. A solid pink tongue is a disqualification. (Tongue colors may lighten due to heat stress; care must be taken not to confuse dilute pigmentation with a pink tongue.)

BODY. *Proportion* — The height of the Shar-Pei from the ground to the withers is approximately equal to the length from the point of breastbone to the point of rump. *Neck* — Medium length, full and set well into the shoulders. There are moderate to heavy folds of loose skin and abundant dewlap about the neck and throat. *Back* — Short and close-coupled, the topline dips slightly behind the withers, slightly rising over the short, broad loin. *Chest* — Broad and deep with the brisket extending to the elbow and rising slightly under the loin. *Croup* — Flat, with the base of the tail set extremely high, clearly exposing an uptilted anus. *Tail* — The high-set tail is a characteristic feature of the Shar-Pei. The tail is thick and round at the base, tapering to a fine point and curling over or to either side of the back. The absence of a complete tail is a disqualification.

FOREQUARTERS. *Shoulders* — Muscular, well laid back and sloping. *Forelegs* — When viewed from the front, straight, moderately spaced, with elbows close to the body. When viewed from the side, the forelegs are straight, the pasterns are strong and flexible. The bone is substantial but never heavy and is of moderate length. *Feet* — Moderate in size, compact and firmly set, not splayed. Removal of front dewclaw is optional.

HINDQUARTERS. Muscular, strong and moderately angulated. The hocks are short, perpendicular to the ground and parallel to each other when viewed from the rear. Hind dewclaws must be removed.

COAT. The extremely harsh coat is one of the distinguishing features of the breed. The coat is absolutely straight and offstanding on the main trunk of the body but generally lies somewhat flatter on the limbs. The coat appears healthy without being shiny or lustrous. Acceptable coat lengths may range from the extremely short "horse coat" up to the "brush coat," not to exceed one inch in length at the withers. A soft coat, a wavy coat, a coat in excess of one inch in length at the withers

Gung Ho's Hot Shot of Top at twelve weeks of age. Owned by Gerald Griffin.

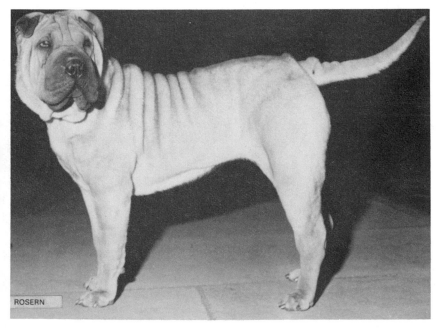

Sedeki's Fab U Lus Flah Beh, a top-winning Chinese Shar-Pei in Great Britain. Bred by Don Wieden. *Rosern Ernie Gascoigne*

Ch. Schmidt's Kan-Pei, owned by Mary Alice Roth.

Ch. ZL's Onlee One Son, owned by Eve Brisack.

or a coat that has been trimmed is a major fault. The Shar-Pei is shown in its natural state.

COLOR. Only solid colors are acceptable. A solid colored dog may have shading, primarily darker shades down the back and on the ears. The shading must be variations of the same body color (except in sables) and may include darker hairs throughout the coat. The following colors are a disqualifying fault: albino, brindle, parti-color (patches), spotted (spots, ticked, roaning) and a tan-pointed pattern (typical black and tan or saddled).

GAIT. The movement of the Shar-Pei is to be judged at a trot. The gait is free and balanced with the feet tending to converge on a centerline of gravity when the dog moves at a vigorous trot. The gait combines good forward reach and a strong drive in the hindquarters. Proper movement is essential.

SIZE. The preferred height is 18 to 20 inches at the withers. The preferred weight is 40 to 55 pounds. The dog is usually larger and more square bodied than the bitch but both appear well proportioned.

TEMPERAMENT. Regal, alert, intelligent, dignified, lordly, scowling, sober and snobbish, essentially independent and somewhat standoffish with strangers, but extreme in his devotion to his family. The Shar-Pei stands firmly on the ground with a calm, confident stature.

Major Faults	**Disqualifying Faults**
1. Deviation from scissors bite	1. Pricked ears
2. Spotted tongue	2. Solid pink tongue
3. A soft coat, a wavy coat, a coat in excess of one inch in length at the withers or a coat that has been trimmed	3. Absence of a complete tail
	4. Not a solid color, i.e., albino, brindle, parti-colored (patches), spotted (including spots, ticked or roaning), tan-pointed pattern (including typical black-and-tan or saddled patterns)

There are other standards for the Chinese Shar-Pei. Each country that recognizes the breed will have its own. Each national club must conform their breed standard to the requirements of the registering organization in their country.

The most frequently used is the FCI standard. The FCI standard is either the standard of record or one on which the club bases their standard. FCI standard No. 309 conforms closely to the original HKKA standard. However, references to fighting dogs or the Chow Chow have been deleted. Also, a much greater height range is allowed than in the other standards. No weight is specified other than that the male is heavier than the bitch.

Standard No. 309   **Native Country: Hong Kong**

ORIGIN AND CHARACTERISTICS.   This authentic Chinese breed has existed for hundreds of years in the provinces bordering on the South China Sea. It appears that the town called "Dah Let" in the province of Kwun Tung must be considered the place of origin.

GENERAL APPEARANCE.   Compact, active, solid and somewhat square built, stands well.

HEAD AND SKULL.   The head large and flat, big in comparison with the body. A number of wrinkles covers the front of the face and the jaws and they are prolonged downwards. The muzzle is fairly large without giving an appearance of shrinking, but more like the muzzle of a hippopotamus.

NOSE.   Black, large and important; occasionally one meets a cream dog with a brick nose and brown dogs with a brown nose but a black nose is preferable.

EYES.   Dark, small and deeply sunk. The beige and cream dogs sometime have lighter colored eyes. The eye is deeply embedded in the wrinkles and covers the front, accentuating even more the melancholy appearance of the dog.

TEETH AND MUZZLE.   Teeth are strong and regular; teeth shut like scissors (firmly). The canine teeth are lightly curved; that is what makes it difficult to remove something that has been picked up. The tongue is rather black. Chops and palate are black. Gums preferably black.

EARS.   Small, narrow, roughly triangular in form, going to a point. They are attached fairly high in the front above the eyes and widely spaced. In certain of these dogs the ears are not so big and only just cover the orifice.

NECK.   Short, narrow, firmly fixed to the shoulders; the skin is in folds around the neck, making large flaps. Shoulders are sloping.

FOREQUARTERS.   Shoulders are sloping and muscular. The front part is straight and fairly long with a solid bone structure.

BODY.   Deep chested, short back; the main line slowly dipping behind, then rising again toward the set of the tail, set very high above the back. In continuation of the wrinkles and dewlaps, numerous pleats of skin overlap the body.

HINDQUARTERS.   The back is strong and muscular. Hocks are fairly open and well hung; leg straight between flanks.

FEET.   Medium, compact and well placed with the toes spread at the joints, which are high and prominent, giving good "aplomb" to the dog.

TAIL.   The tail is rounded at the base and then gets narrower, ending in a fine point. The tail is carried in three positions given below in their order of preference. Most desirable is tail attached high and curved. The second type is carried in a curl, which is quite tight. The third type is curved over the back but without touching it. This allows the dog to wag happily in a very expressive manner. In this and the other cases, the tail should be attached very high, uncovering the back end (anus).

COAT. Specialty of the breed. Coat very short and scratchy; to touch, tough and hard.

COLOR. Black, fire colored, dark brown, beige and cream, very often mixed. The rear end is usually the lightest, without any white marks and never spotted.

WEIGHT AND HEIGHT. 16-20 inches, 40-51 cm. approximately. Male dog heavier than bitch and square. Balance of dog very important.

FAULTS. Splotchy tongue; tail held entirely horizontal or covering anus; a smooth, long, shiny coat and all coats that are not tough and scratchy; a muzzle that is not square enough.

Ch. Ho Wun II, owned by Madeline and Ernest Albright.

57

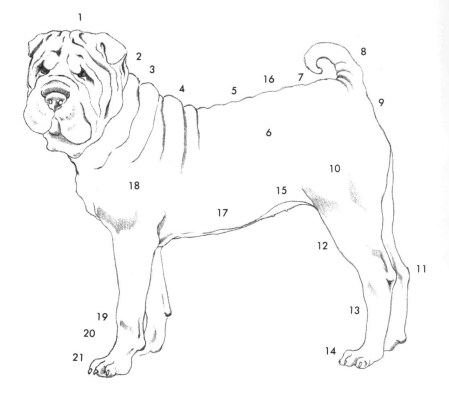

An artistic rendition of the Chinese Shar-Pei standard.

Lynn Travers

1. Head	8. Tail	15. Flank
2. Neck	9. Buttocks	16. Loin Area
3. Collar	10. Thigh	17. Rib Cage
4. Withers	11. Hock	18. Shoulder
5. Back	12. Stifle	19. Wrist
6. Kidney	13. Leg	20. Pastern
7. Croup	14. Foot	21. Toe

5

Interpreting the Chinese Shar-Pei Standard

GENERAL APPEARANCE. An alert, dignified, active, compact dog of medium size and substance, square in profile, close-coupled, the well-proportioned head slightly but not overly large for the body. The short, harsh coat; the loose skin covering the head and body; the small ears; the "hippopotamus" muzzle shape and the high-set tail impart to the Shar-Pei a unique look peculiar to him alone. The loose skin and wrinkles covering the head, neck and body are superabundant in puppies but these features may be limited to the head, neck and withers in the adult.

Comment

The first characteristic to note is the squareness of the body. The Chinese Shar-Pei is compact and short-coupled. The taller dog will be proportionately longer in body, but still square in profile. The Shar-Pei is balanced.

The slightly larger than average head adds rather than detracts from the overall balance. The rise over the loin usually termed the "Trans-Am rear" compensates for the overall dimensions of the head.

No one element of Chinese Shar-Pei anatomy catches the eye more than another. All characteristic Shar-Pei features — from the small ears to the curled tail — contribute to the breed's compactness.

The wrinkling of the Shar-Pei's skin is a unique feature of the breed. Like snowflakes and fingerprints, no two wrinkling patterns are exactly alike. In puppies, the loose skin and folds are superabundant. As the dog matures, they are confined to the head, neck and withers. Adults with loose, saggy skin are incorrect.

Take special note of the combination of the terms *alert* and *dignified*. The Chinese Shar-Pei will animate to a degree. In the presence of strangers, the Shar-Pei is always aloof. Public behavior varies from bored to condescending. The key to animation in this breed is the look in the eyes and the attitude of the body.

> *HEAD.* Large, slightly but not overly, proudly carried and covered with profuse wrinkles on the forehead continuing into side wrinkles framing the face. *Skull* — Flat and broad, the stop moderately defined, the length from nose to stop is approximately the same as from stop to occiput. *Muzzle* — One of the distinctive features of the breed. It is broad and full with no suggestion of snipiness. The lips and top of muzzle are well padded and may cause a slight bulge at the base of the nose. *Nose* — Large and wide and darkly pigmented, preferably black but any color nose conforming to the general coat color of the dog is acceptable. In dilute colors, the preferred nose is self-colored. Darkly pigmented cream Shar-Pei may have some light pigment either in the center of their nose or on their entire nose.

Comment

The Chinese Shar-Pei is a head breed. The shape and features of the head are of major importance to the breed. Each part must complement the others. The head is just as balanced as the body. No one feature attracts the eye more than another.

Three head types are acceptable. Head type depends upon the muzzle and includes bonemouth, classic and meatmouth. Snipy and overdone heads are incorrect.

Bonemouth: A true bonemouth is the most difficult to find. The muzzle is based upon the underlying bone structure, which is broad and full in shape. The padding is light, only about 1/4 inch over the bone. This muzzle will never diminish due to illness or old age.

Classic: The muzzle is moderately heavy and full. Hopefully there is the same solid bone structure under the padding, as in the bonemouth. Here the padding is more dense and provides a heavier, but not overly large head. The muzzle is rounded out by good padding.

Meatmouth: Bone is still the base structure of the muzzle; however, there is a good amount of padding over the bone.

An example of the square profile of a well-built adult male Shar-Pei.

Even as a puppy, the Shar-Pei should have a square profile and a straight front.

61

Desirable head types. Figures A and B denote typical puppy heads at eight and twelve weeks. Figure C is an example of a meatmouth, while Figure D shows the classic head.

C

D

Figure A represents an overdone head. The wrinkling is excessive and the dog would certainly be prone to eye problems due to the heavy folding above the eyes. Figure B represents a dog with a large round eye and startled expression. The ear carriage is incorrect. The dog lacks in muzzle strength and dewlap. Figure C represents the profile of a dog whose muzzle is lacking in depth and fullness. All three represent poor Chinese Shar-Pei heads.

Snipy: The muzzle is narrow and tapering with little bone under the padding. Note that a heavily padded muzzle over narrow bone in puppies can develop into a snipy muzzle in adults. The bone underlying the muzzle in puppies should be only a little narrower than the cheekbone.

Overdone: Definitely too much of a good thing. Breeders don't worry about the bone or symmetry of the head. The padding is extremely heavy and wrinkling is overabundant. The head is overly large for the body.

TEETH — Strong, meeting in a scissors bite. Deviation from a scissors bite is a major fault.

Comment

Bites are especially important in a breed where overdone heads can make a difference. The Chinese Shar-Pei is subject to a condition known as tight lip. In the meatmouth, the lower lip may roll up and over the teeth. Not only can this condition make it difficult to eat, but may push the lower teeth back and cause an overshot bite. The Shar-Pei was designed to be able to hold its prey. A good bite is essential.

EYES — Dark, small, almond shaped and sunken, displaying a scowling expression. In the dilute colored dogs the eye color may be lighter.

Comment

Chinese Shar-Pei eyes are small and deep set. Often the eye is not apparent at first glance. The visibility of the eye depends on whether the dog had entropion, an abnormal condition where the eyelid rolls in toward the eye, and if so how it was corrected. The eyes are dark and contribute to the scowling expression.

EARS — Extremely small, rather thick, equilateral triangles in shape, slightly rounded at the tips, edges of the ear may curl. Ears lie flat against the head, are set wide apart and forward on the skull, pointing toward the eyes. The ears have the ability to move. Pricked ears are a disqualification.

Comment

Note that Shar-Pei can move their ears at will. However, the ears will usually snap back into place at any noise. Small for the head, the ears should not attract undue attention.

TONGUE, ROOF OF MOUTH, GUMS AND FLEWS — Solid bluish-black is preferred in all colors except in dilute colors, which have a solid lavender pigmentation. A spotted tongue is a major fault. A solid pink tongue is

Normal Canine Skull and Dentition

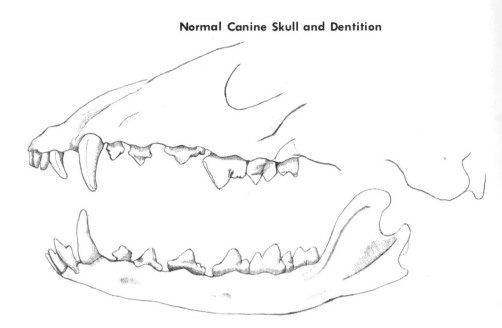

Mouths and Bites

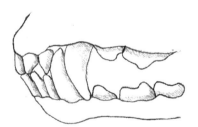

Scissors Bite

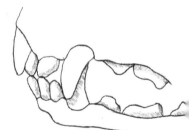

Overshot Bite

Undershot Bite

The bite is important in the Chinese Shar-Pei. The correct bite is scissors. Bites that are undershot or overshot are incorrect no matter the reason.

Ear Set

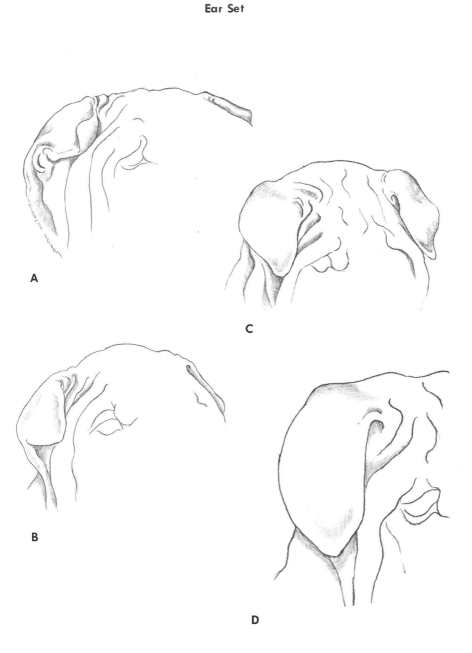

A

C

B

D

Figure A shows the correct ear set of an adult Shar-Pei. Note that some ears will curl slightly at the tip. Figure B shows a puppy ear set. Even though the ear set is correct, a puppy's ears may appear fleshy. Figures C and D show incorrect ear sets. C does not point toward the eye and D is too long.

An example of an incorrect ear set. Note also the large, round eye.

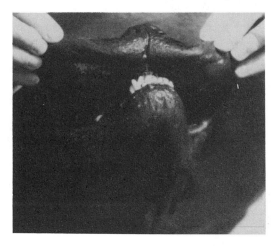

Note the scissor bite and the dark pigmentation of the gums and flews.

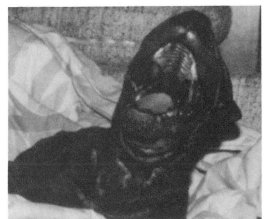

Note the dark pigmentation of the tongue and roof of mouth.

a disqualification. (Tongue colors may lighten due to heat stress; care must be taken not to confuse dilute pigmentation with a pink tongue.)

Comment

The blue-black pigmentation is unique to the Chinese Shar-Pei and the Chow Chow. The color should be uniform. Some puppies may have a slightly spotted or flowered tongue that will fill in completely as the dog matures.

> *BODY.* *Proportion* — The height of a Shar-Pei from the ground to the withers is approximately equal to the length from the point of breastbone to the point of rump. *Neck* — Medium length, full and set well into the shoulders. There are moderate to heavy folds of loose skin and abundant dewlap about the neck and throat. *Back* — Short and close-coupled, the topline dips slightly behind the withers, slightly rising over the short, broad loin. *Chest* — Broad and deep with the brisket extending to the elbow and rising slightly under the loin.

Comment

The Chinese Shar-Pei is square. The dog is well balanced in front and rear. The characteristic topline is important as the *Trans-Am* rear provides balance for the larger head. The back drops slightly at the withers and rises over the loin. Both front and rear quarters are broad and well muscled. Shar-Pei grow quickly but mature slowly. The chest and hips will take time to develop broadness. Adults with a protruding breastbone are incorrect.

> *Croup* — Flat, with the base of the tail set extremely high, clearly exposing an uptilted anus. *Tail* — The high-set tail is a characteristic feature of the Shar-Pei. The tail is thick and round at the base, tapering to a fine point and curling over to either side of the back. The absence of a complete tail is a disqualification.

Comment

The Hong Kong/Kowloon standard defines three correct tail carriages. These are still correct, although not detailed in the current standard.

1. Set on high and curled to either side. Some may be curled so tightly as to form a small ringlet.
2. Curled in a loose ring.
3. Carried high in a curve toward, but not touching, the back.

> *FOREQUARTERS.* *Shoulders* — Muscular, well laid back and sloping. *Forelegs* — When viewed from the front, straight, moderately spaced, with elbows close to the body. When viewed from the side, the forelegs are straight, the pasterns are strong and flexible. The bone is

1. Set High on top in a tight curl. Carried to either side. Correct tail-set.

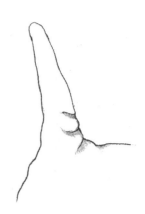

4. Tail carried vertically, a major fault.

2. A loose curl with correct tail-set.

5. Flaccid tail, covering anus — a major fault.

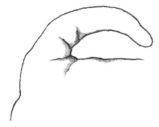

3. Carried high and curved forward. Correct tail-set.

6. Incomplete tail or stub tail — disqualification.

Correct tail-sets are shown in Figures 1, 2 and 3. Incorrect tail-sets shown in Figures 4, 5 and 6.

Toplines

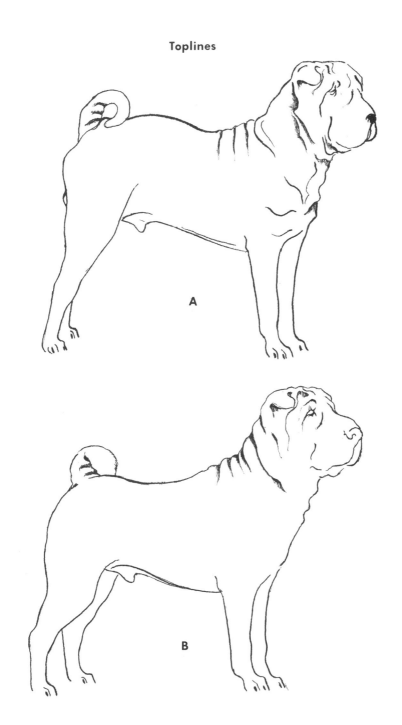

Figure A shows a roached back with a poorly angulated rear. Figure B shows a swayed back, although the rear angulation is good.

Good Front Structure

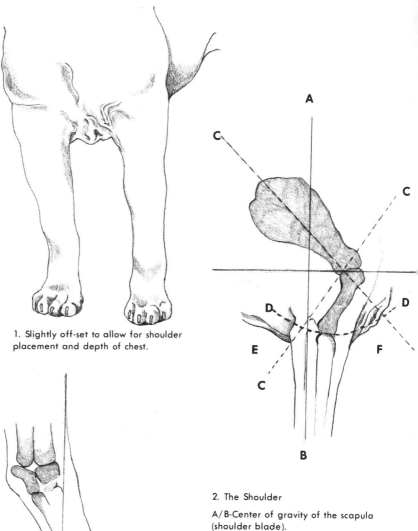

1. Slightly off-set to allow for shoulder placement and depth of chest.

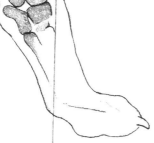

3. The Pastern

A/B-Vertical line with heel pad for static balance. Well-bent pastern; cat foot

2. The Shoulder

A/B-Center of gravity of the scapula (shoulder blade).
C-Correct angulation of the scapula — 45 degrees
D-Arc of the elbow, well-set above the brisket line
E-Well-let-down brisket
F-Chest in front of the leg

72

Good Rear Structure

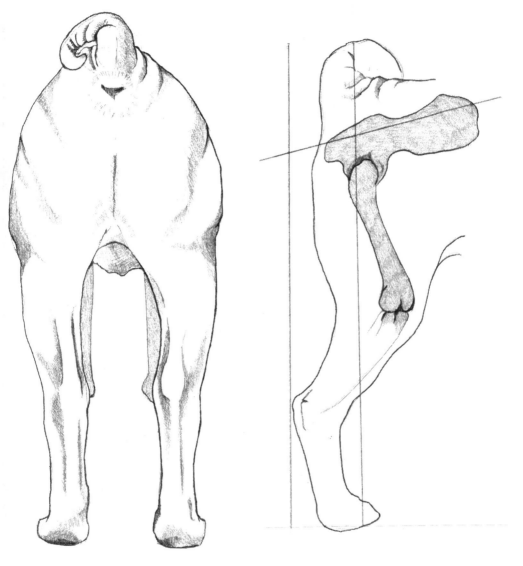

1. Correct rear.

2. Typical angulation in the Chinese Shar-Pei is not so straight in stifle as with the Chow Chow but does deviate from that of most dogs.

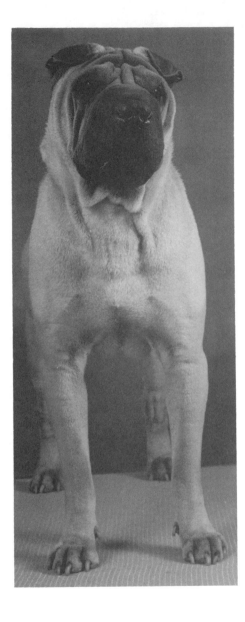

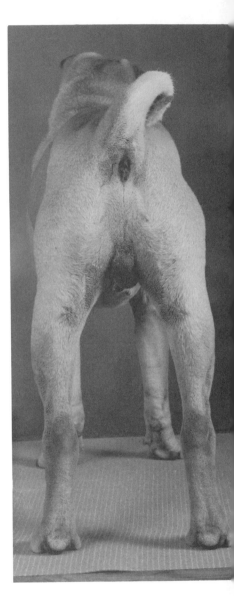

A Photographic study of Chinese Shar-Pei structure from the front, rear and side.
Bruce Harkins

substantial but never heavy and is of moderate length. *Feet* — Moderate in size, compact and firmly set, not splayed. Removal of front dewclaws is optional.

Comment

Fronts are a major problem in Shar-Pei. Good fronts are hard to find. Some bad fronts are genetic, but others develop when a puppy has to support an overly large head. The front bows from the weight.

Note the flexibility of the front pasterns. The leg will curve slightly to act as built-in shock absorbers. The dog is not down in the pasterns.

HINDQUARTERS. Muscular, strong and moderately angulated. The hocks are short, perpendicular to the ground and parallel to each other when viewed from the rear. Hind dewclaws must be removed.

Comment

The rear quarters are moderately angulated. There should be good drive from the hindquarters when moving. Some young dogs have puppy structures around the joint. The hock appears to give, causing an irregular gait. The hock slips out of place, either forward or to the side, when the joint is straightened.

The musculature in the front and rear quarters is well developed. The Shar-Pei is a compact, powerful dog, both when standing and moving.

COAT. The extremely harsh coat is one of the distinguishing features of the breed. The coat is absolutely straight and offstanding on the main trunk of the body but generally lies somewhat flatter on the limbs. The coat appears healthy without being shiny or lustrous. Acceptable coat lengths may range from the extremely short "horse coat" up to the "brush coat," not to exceed one inch in length at the withers. A soft coat, a wavy coat, a coat in excess of one inch in length at the withers or a coat that has been trimmed is a major fault. The Shar-Pei is shown in its natural state.

Comment

The coat is a unique feature of the breed. Matgo Law claims that there are ten types of coat. The CSPCA recognizes three coats:

Horse: The coat is extremely short and harsh. The hair is straight and offstanding from the body. The dog will stiffen the coat even further when upset. Some coats feel like velvet, while others cause Shar-Pei rash. Human skin can be irritated by contact with the harsh, bristly hairs of Shar-Pei. The rash usually disappears with repeated contact with the dog.

Brush: This coat is longer than the horse coat but just as harsh. The hair does not exceed one inch at the withers. The hair at the withers appears longer if wrinkling is present.

Bear: This coat is too long and often soft and/or wavy. Though attractive, the coat is incorrect. Matgo Law's test for a too long coat is to look at the tail. If the tail appears bushy, rather than evenly tapering to a point, the coat is too long.

COLOR. Only solid colors are acceptable. A solid colored dog may have shading, primarily darker shades down the back and on the ears. The shading must be variations of the same body color (except in sables) and may include darker hairs throughout the coat. The following colors are a disqualifying fault: albino, brindle, parti-color (patches) spotted (spots, ticked, roaning) and a tan-pointed pattern (typical black and tan or saddled).

Comment

The key is solid coat coloration. Shading most often appears on horse-coated dogs. Colors are unquestionable in the adult. Puppy coats may change color as the dog matures.

Fawn is the predominant Shar-Pei coat color, ranging from light beige to vibrant red. Cream and black are the next two most prevalent coat colors. Note that cream dogs often have darker ears and shading on the body, with the back being darker than the sides.

Shading is not indicative of a parti-colored dog. Many Shar-Pei have lighter coloring on the underpart of the tail and the back of thighs. Parti-colors are the equivalent of a pinto Akita. The base color is white with colored patches and ticking or spotting.

There are two divisions in Shar-Pei coat colors. Standard colors have black pigmentation. Dilute colors are self-colored, blending with the coat color.

There is some question as to what the Chinese meant by five-point red, but breeders generally accept that it refers to a dog with red pigmentation on the nose, eyes, skin, foot pads and anus. A like coloration is found in the Irish "red nose" family of American Pit Bull Terriers. The coat is a distinct deep red fawn to a dark red color.

The most recently defined color is the silver (dilute). In most other breeds this color is called blue. The coat is a bluish/silverish smokey color that includes blue, grey and taupe.

GAIT. The movement of the Shar-Pei is to be judged at a trot. The gait is free and balanced with the feet tending to converge on a center line of gravity when the dog moves at a vigorous trot. The gait combines good forward reach and a strong drive in the hindquarters. Proper movement is essential.

77

The Chinese Shar-Pei in action. The dog should move at a vigorous trot.

Comment

The Chinese Shar-Pei is a powerful dog meant to move out forcefully. There is good reach in the front quarters and drive in the rear quarters. The Shar-Pei can cover ground quickly, with little effort.

The Shar-Pei *single tracks*, which means that as the speed increases, the legs converge on a center line of gravity. The AKC defines single tracking as: "All footprints falling on a single line of travel. When a dog breaks into a trot, his body is supported by only two legs at a time, which move as alternating diagonal pairs. To achieve balance, his legs angle inward toward a center line beneath his body and the greater the speed, the closer they come to tracking on a single line."

SIZE. The preferred height is 18 to 20 inches at the withers. The preferred weight is 40 to 55 pounds. The dog is usually larger and more square bodied than the bitch but both appear well proportioned.

Comment

Throughout all the standard changes, the height has not varied. However, the preferred weight has gone up and down, mostly up. The average Shar-Pei currently weighs 45-50 pounds, with the standard allowing 40-55 pounds. Weight should be in proportion to height, giving a solid, square-bodied appearance. The Chinese Shar-Pei's bulk depends on muscle tone. A flabby dog is incorrect even if he falls within the preferred weight range. Though the male Shar-Pei is larger and more square bodied than the female, the difference between the sexes is not dramatic.

TEMPERAMENT. Regal, alert, intelligent, dignified, lordly, scowling, sober and snobbish, essentially independent and somewhat standoffish with strangers, but extreme in his devotion to his family. The Shar-Pei stands firmly on the ground with a calm, confident stature.

Comment

The term regal best describes the Chinese Shar-Pei when in public. They are standoffish with strangers, appearing bored or snobbish. Don't be put off by the aloof attitude when you first meet a Shar-Pei. Look at their eyes for a mischevious spark and the tentative wag of the tail from barely controlled enthusiasm. At home, Shar-Pei are born clowns, enthusiastic, loving and entertaining.

Major Faults	Disqualifying Faults
1. Deviation from a scissors bite	1. Pricked ears
2. Spotted tongue	2. Solid pink tongue
3. A soft coat, a wavy coat, a coat in excess of one inch in length at the withers or a coat that has been trimmed.	3. Absence of a complete tail
	4. Not a solid color, i.e., albino, brindle, parti-colored (patches), spotted (including spots, ticked or roaning), tan-pointed pattern (including typical black-and-tan or saddled patterns)

Comment

Disqualifying faults are features totally unacceptable in the Chinese Shar-Pei. Any dog with any of the faults listed cannot be shown in conformation competition. If a Shar-Pei with a disqualifying fault is entered in a show, the judge will disqualify the dog and ask the handler to remove the entry from the ring.

Major faults do not ban the dog from conformation competition. You may enter the dog and it will not be excused from the ring for that fault. However, dogs with major faults usually don't win, as they exhibit features that are undesirable in the Shar-Pei.

COAT COLORS (VISUAL), AS RECOGNIZED BY THE REGISTRAR

In relation to the standard of the breed, no one solid coat color is preferred over any other solid color.

The variations in coat colors as described below do not alter the color requirements or preferences as described in the standard of the breed.

Group A: Basic Colors

Has black (charcoal) pigmentation, i.e. skin, nose, tongue, mouth/flews and foot pads. Nails may be lighter.

Group B: Dilute Colors

No black (charcoal) pigmentation anywhere on dog. Skin, nose and nails are self-colored blending with the coat color. Eyes may be light or dark. Tongues may vary from light to dark lavender.

CREAM.   An "off white" color. May have darker ears and shading along the dorsal line. May be described as light cream, cream or dark cream.

80

CREAM (DILUTE).　　An "off white" color. May have darker shading on the ears and along the dorsal line. May be described as light cream, cream or dark cream.

FAWN.　　A very light tan/golden color ranging to a dark tan/golden. Some fawns with dark fawn coats have a pronounced red tinge. May have darker shading along the dorsal line. Red fawns may have lighter colored skin, eyes and toe nails. They should have a solid colored nose and foot pads. May be described as light fawn, fawn, dark fawn or red fawn.

APRICOT (DILUTE).　　Similar to but lighter in color than five-point red (dilute). A distinct apricot color ranging in shades from light to dark apricot.

RED.　　Mahogany to rich chestnut red (example: Irish Setter). The coat color is uniform over the body, neck, head and legs. Very little variation.

FIVE-POINT RED (DILUTE).　　A distinct deep red fawn varying to a dark red color. The coat color is uniform over the body, neck, head and legs. Very little variation. The "five points" are nose, eyes, skin, foot pads and anus.

BROWN.　　Medium to dark brown color. The coat color is uniform over the body, neck, head and legs. Very little variation.

CHOCOLATE.　　A medium to dark color (example: milk or dark chocolate). The coat color is uniform over the body, neck, head and legs. Includes liver.

SABLE.　　A lacing of black hairs over a lighter ground color. Two separate colored hairs — one black and one a lighter color (not white). The coat color is uniform over the body, neck and head and legs. Very little variation.

SABLE (DILUTE).　　A lacing of dark colored hair over a lighter colored ground color. Two separate colored hairs — one dark (red, brown, silver) and one a lighter color (not white). The coat color is uniform over the body, neck, head and legs. Very little variation.

BLACK.　　True black. May have a blue, grey, brown or red tinge on the sides. The coat color is uniform over the body, neck, head and legs. Very little variation. May bleach, fade or brown from exposure to the sun.

SILVER (DILUTE).　　Includes blue, grey and taupe. A bluish/silverish smokey color. The coat color is uniform over the body, neck, head and legs. Very little variation. Nose is slate. Mouth/tongue is lavender. Skin, eyes, foot pads and nails are self-colored.

Group C: Not a Solid Colored Coat

ALBINO.

BRINDLE.   A fine mixture of black hairs with hairs of a lighter color, usually tan, brown or grey with typical tiger stripe pattern.

PARTI-COLOR.   Variegated in patches of two or more colors.

SPOTTED.   Spots, ticked or roaning.

TAN-POINTED PATTERN.   Such as commonly found in black and tan, liver and tan (Doberman Pinscher) or saddle pattern (German Shepherd). These patterns or variations may appear in other combinations.

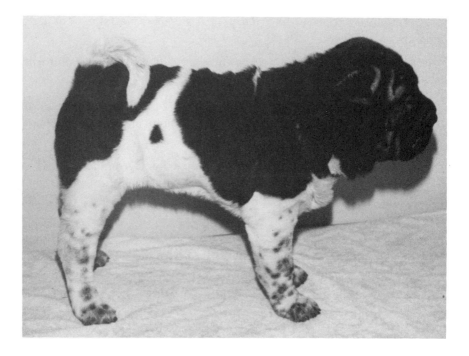

An example of a flowered or spotted puppy.

6

Character of the
Chinese Shar-Pei

THE OFFICIAL STANDARD describes the Chinese Shar-Pei as a dog that "stands firmly on the ground with a calm, confident stature." Adjectives describing his demeanor include "regal, alert, intelligent, dignified, lordly, scowling, sober and snobbish."

Such is the impression the Shar-Pei gives when he dons his public face. He remains aloof with strangers. He accepts pats and compliments as if they were his by right. He maintains an arrogance that places him above the hulabaloo taking place around him. Essentially, he has a quiet dignity that belies the fact that he is a born clown.

The Chinese Shar-Pei has many faces that he dons at will. The breed is deceptive when seen only at shows. No one should assume he understands Shar-Pei until he has experienced them in their home environment.

The personality of each Shar-Pei is as unique as his appearance. Each one is different in temperament and function.

The Shar-Pei was developed as and remains a multipurpose dog. He has been used for guarding, hunting and herding. These instincts are still strong.

The Shar-Pei is "extreme in his devotion to his family." He enjoys human contact. In any multiple Shar-Pei household, at least one dog will take the job of keeping his environment secure. One or more dogs will respond to strange sounds. A sleeping Shar-Pei can become instantly awake and alert at the least disturbance.

His exceptional eyesight allows him to keep a vigilant watch over his property. Though primarily a property guardian, he will also protect his owner much in the manner of the Mastiff. He is quick and agile, capable of stepping in between his owner and any perceived threat. His "Trans-Am" rear is ideal for butting another dog out of the way. If this proves insufficient to repel the threat, he will warn before proceeding further. In most cases he will try to pin rather than bite.

On the whole, the Chinese Shar-Pei is not an aggressive dog. Rather, he is a thinking animal who must be allowed to assess the situation and make up his own mind as to the appropriate reaction. The job of the Shar-Pei owner is to teach the dog good judgment.

The Shar-Pei is not aggressive without cause. However, it must be understood that many Shar-Pei consider themselves *alpha* or dominant and do not take kindly to being stared down by another dog. This is perceived as an act of aggression. This tendency, combined with his possible fighting-dog heritage, has led some to consider the breed bad tempered. Consider that in China all guard dogs are called fighting dogs. The Shar-Pei is only doing the job his instincts demand.

Chinese Shar-Pei do not need any training to act as a guard dog. Neither does the breed need training to hunt or herd.

Shar-Pei exhibit quiet patience and exceptional eyesight, traits that come into play when stalking their prey. Many Shar-Pei can catch a mouse or other small animal better than felines.

The herding instinct is most often evident when younger dogs or small children are in the house. The Shar-Pei feels he has to guard these defenseless beings and can only do so if they are in a group. He is a great babysitter.

The Shar-Pei loves children. He will accept any amount of handling and playing from a child, and will submit to indecencies he would find embarrassing under other circumstances. The same is basically true with puppies, although he will set limits and discipline offenders when puppy antics get out of hand.

From puppy to adult, a Shar-Pei is inventive and will provide hours of entertainment for his human companions. No barrier is too strong or object too common for a Chinese Shar-Pei in pursuit of fun and games.

Some favorite games of the Shar-Pei are "chew face" and "chew foot." Chew face occurs when one Shar-Pei latches onto the flews or muzzle of another dog. It is a benign, ritualistic game. When a puppy plays with an adult this may result in the younger dog hanging suspended from the older dog's neck. With adults the results are usually noisy, as they talk to each other. Of course turnabout is fair play, and the original instigator will find his muzzle in the other dog's mouth. Chew foot is a variation on the same theme. One dog pounces on another, taking a leg in his mouth, usually a

Even at eight weeks of age Bonnie knew she was destined for stardom and it shows.
Muller Studio

A prelude to their favorite game — chew face.

rear leg. The point is to bring the other dog down to the ground as quickly as possible. This creates some interesting dance steps as one dog tries to evade the other and take his turn at chew foot.

Chew face and chew foot appear to be universal Shar-Pei activities. Other antics vary from dog to dog.

A VISIT TO A CHINESE SHAR-PEI FAMILY

From the minute you arrive at Gung Ho Chinese Shar-Pei you are deluged in wrinkled dogs. Six may not seem like many until they all start meeting and greeting you at one time. The enthusiasm is contagious, and each one must have his or her rightful share. If one dog feels left out, he will simply hop up and use his rump to butt the offending animal out of the way. Thus having removed the competition, he will walk up proudly for his just reward. Many a bruise has been delivered by an eager Shar-Pei.

Most breeders are well aware that a typical Shar-Pei greeting can be overwhelming to the uninitiated and will limit the number of dogs out at one time. However, I asked for the full treatment, and the hooligans happily complied.

Their public demeanor was nowhere to be seen. This was their home, and an extra person only provided a greater audience. Dog shows are nice, but home is a Shar-Pei's castle.

At Gung Ho, Ch. Bruce Lee's Bonnie Brenna is the unchallenged queen — Cleopatra style. Her regal attitude has helped make her one of the top-winning Shar-Pei bitches in the country. This same demeanor carries over into the home. No one disturbs Bonnie's beauty rest and no dog would dare put his paws on Bonnie's back. She is a dominant bitch who prefers to be above the rest of the crowd.

Bonnie can be a terror or an angel all at the same time. She can strike as fast as a viper at an upstart and has been known to hiss like a cat. However, in a minute she can become a beatific vision, cuddling up to her owner or a favored visitor, patting an arm with a forepaw and wearing her "butter wouldn't melt in my mouth" face.

Bonnie is the playmaker. She'll start the game and will play until she's tired or bored. Then the rest can continue the game, as long as she is not disturbed. Though she and the other dogs usually prefer games that require two or more to play, Bonnie can entertain herself if necessary.

Bonnie's best antic to date is her pillow dance. From one end of the room to the other, Bonnie gracefully dances, picking up one pillow after another, effortlessly tossing each into the air. Peg Kastner reports that Bonnie's son, Ch. Gung Ho's Eminent Domain, performs the same pillow dance when he has nothing else to do. The other dogs find the dance

The welcoming committee at Gung Ho Rare Chinese Shar-Pei.

Ch. Hillie's Roisin Rua-Gung Ho still looks as innocent as an adult as she did as a puppy.
Bob Barber

Ch. Bruce Lee's Rumpole De Ruga at eleven weeks of age.

fascinating, swinging their heads back and forth like fans at a tennis match.

As there is only one Bonnie, the other two girls have developed their own specialties.

Ch. Hillie's Roisin Rua-Gung Ho, better known as Rosie, is a trooper. Subjected to much mothering by LuLu as a puppy, she remains "Daddy's girl." A deviation from the black brush coat tradition at Gung Ho, her brilliant red color has made her a favorite with the photographers.

Rosie has made her mark on the show world in the junior handling ring. Rosie is self-assured and confident. However, she is not arrogant and easily slips into her role of inveterate clown at home.

The youngest of the females, Rosie often enlists the aid of Jiggs, the youngest male. She is the major instigator of chew face and chew foot. She has been known to take these games one step further and plays chew ear, much to the dismay of her stage mother, Alice Lawlor, who does not want her dogs to have ragged ears. No matter what mischief she causes, Rosie always looks the innocent.

Finally, the last but not least of the girls is LuLu. LuLu is a big girl with the grace of a ballerina. No gate is too high, no barrier to food too formidable for her. If allowed, she'd eat herself into oblivion.

LuLu loves puppies and will do anything to initiate the latest addition into the pack. She will tolerate any amount of abuse from the little ones. LuLu spent Rosie's first year in the household with Rosie hanging from her jowls. She happily babysits when the other dogs get tired of puppy antics.

Three girls are plenty to keep up with, since the female Shar-Pei is often more dominant than the male. The male tends to have a more passive temperament and is slower to mature. However, these are variables and a dog with a seemingly soft temperament can still be thick-headed — as can be all Shar-Pei. Though they want to please and can be quite easily trained for obedience, as a breed they are stubborn. However, if they weren't a thinking breed, half the fun and all the chaos a Shar-Pei can create would be lost.

With all the activity, disagreements invariably arise. Therefore, each household needs an enforcer to leave the owners' time to themselves (of course, it can be debated whether Shar-Pei are the owned or the owners).

At Gung Ho, Ch. Bruce Lee's Rumpole de Ruga is the enforcer. Expert at wielding his rump, Rumpole breaks up the disagreeing parties. He walks in between the two and looks from side to side as if to say, "How dare you create a disturbance in this house!" One look is often sufficient, but if stronger measures are needed a well-placed bump will usually break up the confrontation. As the "muscle man" of the group, it is only right that Rumpole should take the role of a bouncer. Oddly enough, Rumpole is the favorite dog of Alice's Persian cats, who often lie down with him for a nap.

A Stage Mother is born. Alice Lawler is shown with puppy Rosie and her traveling billboard. *Bob Barber*

L'il Lulu of Gung Ho looking for a puppy to mother.

Gerard Studio

90

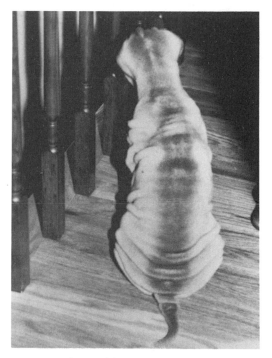

Waiting for Daddy to come home. Shongum's Honeybear, owned by Alicia Kastner.

The Gung Ho Gang in a long down.

"Gotta Get a Little Gung Ho at Christmas." Ch. Gung Ho's Captain Jiggs and Ch. Hillies Roisin Rua-Gung Ho. *Bob Barber*

When not keeping the peace, Rumpole is the favorite "meeter and greeter" of the neighborhood. He loves to meet new people and happily washes everyone's face. He delivers what his owner calls "head-rocking" kisses.

Face washing is a favorite Shar-Pei habit. Some will lick from chin to forehead while others prefer to give little love nips, primarily on the chin. Face washing extends to dogs as well as humans. The males at Gung Ho wash each other's faces every morning. It is also a sign that a male has been accepted as an adult when the others start washing his face in the morning.

Face washing, chew games and rump bumping are all performed as a sort of Shar-Pei ritual, at which Rumpole is the expert. Even his breeding behavior reeks of ceremony. He's fascinating to watch as he dances, postures and snorts in an effort to impress a lady.

Ch. Aja's Gung Ho of Bucklee, on the other hand, has little use for mating ritual. After his brief tap dance and serenade, he's all business and never misses the mark.

Gung Ho likes the quiet life and is a man of few words. Alice fancies him the "Fred Astaire" of the dog world. He is agile and appears to levitate up staircases. Though willing to join in the games, he doesn't like the play to get too rough. One quick grunt is all he needs to calm an offender.

His grunt also serves to express his displeasure about unpleasant circumstances. When asked to enter his crate, he has to have the last word. Halfway inside he'll grunt and then proceed in all the way to settle down for a rest. Once he forgot to have his say and backed out halfway to grunt before going back into the crate without argument.

Last but not least is Ch. Gung Ho's Captain Jiggs. Jiggs is a testament to the slow maturation of some Shar-Pei males. Though his body is mature, Alice claims he is still "out to lunch." Unpredictable, embarrassing moments can occur at anytime, as Jiggs tends to barrel into situations better left alone. He creates more work for the enforcer and will sometimes sustain the wrath of an offended dog. Jiggs is the baby, or so we think. Quite possibly he has everyone fooled into allowing him greater latitude for his antics.

A day at Gung Ho is eventful. There is plenty of activity, but there are periods of relative quiet when everyone takes a rest. I say relative quiet because, as we all soon learn, Chinese Shar-Pei snore loudly!

No wonder owners of Chinese Shar-Pei say "They are like potato chips. It is hard to stop at one."

COMMUNITY RELATIONSHIPS

The Shar-Pei can live amicably with each other and with other animals. The trick is to bring in puppies with the adults. As the puppy grows up, he

A meeting of the Oriental minds. Gung Ho's Hot Shot of TOP takes a break from fun and games with Ichiban's Keiko Hoshi No Wicca, a two-year-old Akita. Both are owned by Gerry and Linda Griffin.

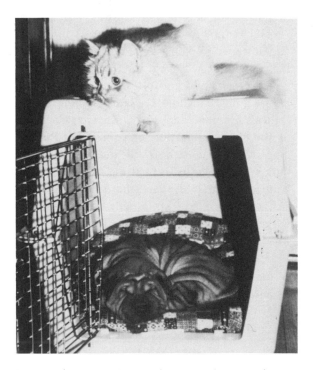

Jennyanydots, a Persian cat, keeps watch over a sleeping Shar-Pei puppy.

At least one Shar-Pei has gone to the birds.

Ch. Schmidt's Kan-Pei with friend. Both reside with Mary Alice Roth in Pennsylvania.

integrates into the pack slowly. It is best to introduce puppies to the pack at varying times. Puppies from the same litter or of the same approximate age can sometimes be too rough on each other. If one dog is older, he can put an end to unruly activity. This gives the new pup needed discipline, which helps pave the way to acceptance as an adult.

Other breeds get along with a Shar-Pei, again, as long as the new dog is brought in as a young puppy. An older dog that is unaware of the joys a Shar-Pei finds in chew games will generally be tolerant with a young dog, and may even learn to play the game. Shar-Pei have been successfully integrated with Akitas, Rottweilers, Samoyeds, West Highland White Terriers, Shiba Inu and many other purebred and mixed breed dogs.

At some point the dogs may instigate a reordering of the pack, which is usually resolved in its own time. Such posturing is more prevalent with females than males. However, such disagreements may erupt among the stud dogs when a bitch is in for breeding. But once the object of disagreement goes home or comes out of season, the status quo is reestablished.

The males seem more willing to take life as it comes. Females are more prone to argument and will hold a grudge. Human intervention may be necessary to keep peace.

Other pets are acceptable to Shar-Pei. Some they ignore, others provide oppotunity for fun and games. For example, a cat who meanders through the house ignoring the dogs is usually ignored by the Shar-Pei. However, a cat who makes quick movements will usually be chased. It all depends on the behavior of the other animal.

Pets that the Shar-Pei might consider prey are not encouraged. White mice, small rabbits or hamsters could bring out the hunting instinct in the dog and such pets would need to be confined out of Shar-Pei reach.

Shar-Pei also have a fascination with objects that swing. This includes such items as horse, dog and cat tails. Chasing or biting another animal's tail must be discouraged in the puppy. What can be cute in a puppy could be devastating behavior in an adult dog, especially one as powerful as the Chinese Shar-Pei. Be careful if another animal with a swinging tail is brought in with Shar-Pei.

Most problems can be prevented by proper socialization. Socializing a dog means taking him out to meet people and other animals. The more situations a young dog is exposed to and adjusts to, the less likelihood there is of a problem emerging at a later date. Once a dog learns good judgment, he can face almost any situation confidently. Remember the Chinese Shar-Pei is a thinking dog and bases his reaction on experience.

96

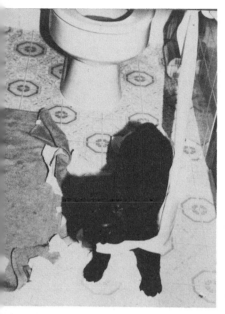

Fingertail Teaberry H.O.T. at play.
Owners: Barbara and Gary Roche.

Ch. Aja's Gung Ho of Bucklee demonstrates a favorite pastime of both his mother and his daughter.

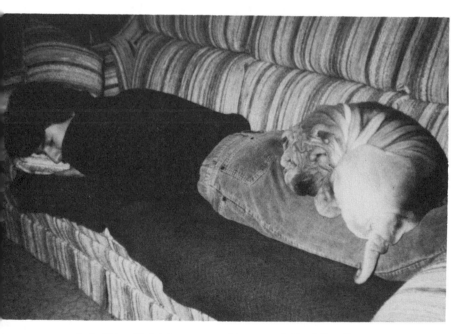

L. F. China Doll takes a nap with owner Michael Fiorella.

In dealing with the Shar-Pei, "kindergarten" puppy training (KPT) and formal obedience classes are highly recommended. They will help you to understand your dog's behavior and resolve any problem areas early. The Chinese Shar-Pei is an expert at psychology. He will finagle his way into your heart and take over before you know what has happened.

Ch. Bruce Lee's Kilo Tu Yang loves to play in the snow. Owner: Vivien Kelly.

7

Selecting a Chinese
Shar-Pei Puppy

SELECTING A SHAR-PEI puppy should involve a lot
of thought and some investigation. The Chinese Shar-Pei is not a stuffed
toy. No matter how cute and cuddly he appears, the Shar-Pei is still a dog
with all the needs of any other breed.

You are making a major commitment of time and resources. Chinese
Shar-Pei live an estimated 12 to 15 years; the oldest to date died one week
short of 19 years. During his life he will be totally dependent on you for his
health and happiness. In addition, a Shar-Pei puppy is not cheap. Where
some puppies can be purchased for a few hundred dollars, most well-bred
Shar-Pei puppies run into the thousands. This is especially true if you are
interested in a show prospect or pick of the litter.

Before making up your mind, educate yourself about the breed. Learn
all the idiosyncracies common to the Chinese Shar-Pei and be sure the
Shar-Pei temperament is compatible with your life style. Not everyone can
deal with every breed.

Some things to consider:

1. The Shar-Pei have a harsh coat. Handling some Shar-Pei can
   cause "Shar-Pei rash" in certain individuals. This condition
   usually disappears with continued exposure. It does not occur
   with every dog you touch and isn't coat specific.
2. Many Shar-Pei slobber when they are hot or excited.
3. Many Shar-Pei develop entropion, a turning in of the eyelid
   that may have to be surgically corrected.
4. Shar-Pei snort and snore.

Khan-Du puppies, owned by Elly Paulus.

Fingertail Teaberry H.O.T. as a puppy, owned by Barbara and Gary Roche.

Xanadu Chi, a horse-coated puppy owne by Barbara Wainer, and Xanadu Raisin, brush-coated puppy owned by Ellen a John Moller.

On the positive side, Shar-Pei shed very little, housebreak themselves, do not smell and are devoted companions.

All things considered, you may still decide you want a Chinese Shar-Pei. You must then decide if you want a pet or a puppy with show potential.

A puppy with show potential is one the breeder believes will mature into an excellent specimen of the breed. As a puppy he comes as close to the written breed standard as possible. While it is true that there are no perfect dogs, some come closer to the standard than others. Don't let a breeder tell you the puppy is a guaranteed show dog. At eight weeks, the puppy may be outstanding, but much can happen between eight weeks and adulthood. You have to take your chances, give him the best care and hope he realizes his potential.

A pet-quality dog can be a good example of the breed, but he usually has one or more points that fall short of breeder expectations. These may be major or minor points that determine whether the dog should not be shown and/or bred. In some cases breeders will insist on a spay/neuter contract. They will withhold the registration papers until proof is presented that the dog has been neutered. The Chinese Shar-Pei Club of America provides an option for placing the letters NB (not for breeding) on the permanent registration papers of physically faulty dogs.

Whether you are searching for a show dog or a pet, the animal should be physically and emotionally sound. All puppies are adorable, but they also all grow up. You want to be as happy with your adult dog as you were with your puppy.

The first step is to find a responsible breeder. The CSPCA maintains a list of active members and clubs in your area. The local club usually has a list of litters available. Advertisements in magazines such as *The Barker, Orient Express II* and *Dog World* announce expected litters and show pictures of adult dogs or puppies from previous litters. *The Barker* and *The Orient Express II* are especially helpful, as they also provide up-to-date breed information. However, the fact that certain breeders advertise does not assure quality or mean they have what you are looking for in a puppy.

Another source of information and breeders is a dog show. Whenever you see a listing for *rare breeds invited* there will usually be Chinese Shar-Pei in attendance. This is ideal because you will see multiple dogs and get a chance to talk to people active in the breed.

Each kennel's dogs have a look. Some may appeal to you more than others. Certain kennels breed primarily for horse coat, others for brush. Color may also be kennel-specific, though color alone should not be a

Ch. Bruce Lee's Wrinky Lee with six-week-old puppies. Bred and owned by Linda and Mike Schatzburg.   *Crezentia*

A four-month-old black puppy owned by Mary Ann Smithers.

A litter of black puppies admiring the camera. From left to right: Ch. Gung Ho's Eminent Domain, owned by Peg Kastner; Ch. Gung Ho's Madame Yoko Ono Li, owned by Susan Kasoff; and Ch. Gung Ho's Captain Jiggs, owned by Alice Lawler.   *Bob Barber*

Puppies from Shoestring Acres, owned by Zell Llewellyn.

determining factor in selecting a puppy. These items may limit your selection of a breeder.

Finally, you can investigate ads in the local newspaper. This should be the last resort, however, as both reputable breeders and backyard breeders (those with one or two dogs who decide to have a litter without the knowledge or experience necessary) advertise. It will be up to you to evaluate the quality of the puppy. Unless you have experience in other breeds, newspaper advertisements are not a good source for selecting your first dog. As you gain experience you may be able to buy dogs sight unseen because you know the pedigrees and trust specific breeders to send you what you want.

Armed with names, addresses and phone numers, your shopping can begin. Call the breeders you are interested in visiting. Talk with them about their dogs, their breeding program, puppies available and what they offer as terms and guarantees. Due to the high purchase price, breeders will sometimes offer a term contract for a good home. This may include stud rights or puppies back in exchange for a lower up-front cost. Be sure you are willing to fulfill a long-term agreement and get along well with the breeder before entering into any of these contracts. Be specific in what you are looking to own. Don't terminate the conversation if they don't have what you want. All information is valuable, and most breeders love to talk about their dogs. These conversations will also give you an idea of what others are offering. When you find the breeder with whom you want to deal, he or she may have puppies available or may have something for you later.

Beware of breeders who claim to have the best without documentation to back it up. Breeders should be willing to discuss their problems as well as their successes.

Expect questions about your home and life style. Breeders are concerned about where their puppies go. Many like to keep track of them as they grow and develop.

Once you find one or more breeders that have or expect to have what you want, arrange for a visit. Prepare beforehand any questions you want to ask. Decide whether you want to visit one or several breeders before you buy. Determine to be open and honest with the people you meet. Good communication can prevent later problems and misunderstandings. Most of all, steel yourself not to fall in love and buy the first wrinkled wonder you see. This is hard with Shar-Pei because they are all cute. No other breed can tug at the heart strings quite like a Chinese Shar-Pei.

While visiting the breeders ask to see the sire and dam. If one or both parents are not in residence, ask to see pictures. This will indicate how your

Puppies at Joss Kennels. Owner: Kandi Stirling.

A black and a cream puppy at Joss Kennels.
Owner: Kandi Stirling

A basket of puppies bred by Greg Masters. From left to right: Gung Ho's Hot Shot of TOP, MP Gung Ho's Ping Ki Li and MP Gung Ho's Blue Jasper. Hot Shot is owned by Gerry Griffin and the other two are owned by Peg Kastner. *Bob Barber*

Ch. Hillie's Roisin Rua-Gung Ho at eight weeks of age.

puppy will look as an adult. If possible, view other offspring of the same sire and dam. The more dogs you see, the better will be your understanding of what that kennel is producing.

During your evaluation, bear in mind that whelping is not kind to the female Shar-Pei. She may look moth eaten or generally in poor condition. Remember puppies are a tremendous drain on the dam. At eight weeks when prospective owners arrive she is at her worst.

Ask about any problems the breeders have experienced. Specifically inquire about general health, skin problems, eye problems and hip dysplasia.

Get specific details about sales contracts, terms (if available) and guarantees. Most breeders guarantee the puppy's health for a period of time. Find out if the puppy has had entropion and, if so, how it was corrected.

Getting all the pertinent facts can be accomplished at one time or spread out through your visit. It depends on the breeder. Some like to sit down and talk. Others carry on a running conversation as you take a tour of the dogs.

You may be presented with one or more puppies to consider. A breeder will not usually bring out his show prospect if he knows you want a pet, and vice versa. The more puppies you see the better you can evaluate their interaction.

If you can't see a number of puppies, an alternative evaluation method is Puppy Aptitude Testing (PAT), where certain instincts and skills are evaluated through simple tests. Some breeders use it to match puppies to new owners. They can determine which puppy is more dominant, which is more outgoing, etc. This assures you of a puppy suited to our temperament and life style. Again, be specific about what you want and honest in answering questions.

Evaluate the puppies presented point by point. Forget the wrinkles and cuteness; look at the dog.

When considering a show prospect look for a solid, well-built puppy. The profile should be square. The back should be short, legs straight and as long as his body. The head should be somewhat large for the body, but still give a sense of balance. Your eye should travel from front to rear without any one aspect of the dog attracting more attention than another. If one point strikes you, examine that aspect carefully. There may be a problem, depending upon the age of the animal. Older puppies and adolescents grow in stages. There will be periods where the dog lacks balance.

After assessing the health of the dog and gaining a general impression of the puppy, examine each point described in the standard.

Bruce Lee's Nikki Sulee at three months of age. Owner: Theresa Stewart.

Wrinkled son of Ch. Peppermint Man Joss, owned by Kandi Stirling.

A three-month-old puppy owned by Kandi Stirling.

The head is an important aspect of breed type. The skull is flat and broad. The muzzle is broad and full with a bulge at the base of the nose. The puppy bulge is more defined than that of an adult and resembles a lima bean. The lips and top of the muzzle are well padded. When viewed from the front the lower jaw appears wider than the top jaw. Wrinkling is profuse on the forehead and cheeks. However, moderation in all things is essential. Too much wrinkling on the face leads to eye problems, tight lips and a saggy appearance as an adult. You should be able to see the eyes, which are small, dark and sunken. The ears are small equilateral triangles held close to the head. When in their proper position, the ears will point toward the eyes. Remember, the ears are mobile. Whistle at the puppy to gain its attention and get the ears positioned properly.

Always check the bite and mouth. The lips should roll back easily to reveal the teeth and gums. Some puppies suffer from tight lip, where the lower lip is held tightly on or over the lower teeth. This can cause misalignment of the bite, as well as eating problems. The bite should be scissored. The tongue is a distinctive blue-black. Shar-Pei are born with pink tongues, which darken as the dog ages. A few pink spots in a young puppy may fill in as he matures, but the greater the flowering or spotting, the less likely the tongue will fill in completely. The roof of the mouth, gums and flews should also indicate solid blue-black pigmentation upon maturity. Dogs with dilute coat colors will have lavender pigmentation. Check the color code chart for definitions of proper coloration and pigmentation.

Feel the coat. It should be harsh. Horse coats are short and the hair lies close to the body. The dog appears to be clothed in a velvet nap. Brush coats are slightly longer, though no more than one inch at the withers, the highest point of the shoulders. All coats appear longer and stand off the body at the withers due to wrinkling over the shoulders. Check between wrinkles and toes for signs of irritation

The coat should be a solid color, with some shading allowed. This shading will usually be darker down the back and over the ears. It is not always possible to determine the adult coat in a puppy. The breeder should be able to tell you what he expects the color to become, but the final result will not be certain until the animal is six months of age — and there may still be some subtle changes up to one year of age.

The legs should be straight. The forelegs are moderately spaced with the elbows close to the body. The slope of the front pastern is distinctive. This allows the legs to act as shock absorbers. The Shar-Pei is a powerful, muscular dog capable of vigorous movement. Without the slope of the pastern, the impact would be absorbed by the shoulders, to the detriment

Shar-Pei grow quickly, as evidenced by the three-week difference in ages between these two puppies.

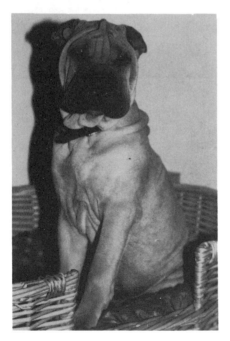

So-Ying's J.S. Bok, owned by William Glazer, Alfonso Sobelli and Christopher J. Volker.

Sui Yeen's Tisa Moon Yang, bred by Rose Ellen and Morgan Stone.

Windsong's Mimosa, owned by Edie Buchko.

of the animal. The bone is substantial but never heavy. Again, the key word is *moderation.*

The rear is heavily muscled, but moderate in angulation and bone. The hocks are short and perpendicular to the ground. The feet are moderate in size; the toes are compact and firm. There should be no signs of splaying. Nails must be kept short to maintain the tight foot. The puppy may have front dewclaws but rear dewclaws should be removed (most puppies are born without rear dewclaws, however).

Watch the puppy move. The gait will be loose and the body will tend to roll slightly. However, movement should be smooth and effortless even at this young age.

Check the tail set. The tail is thick and round at the base, tapering to a fine point. The most desirable tail is set on high and curled over the back to either side. Puppy tails rarely curl this early. The second type of tail is curled in a loose ring. The third type is curved toward, but not touching, the back. On any dog the tail should be set high, showing the anus.

Finally, compare the puppy to the standard for any faults or disqualifications. Assuming all is well, step back and get another general impression of the puppy. Has your opinion changed? If not, you are probably looking at a good puppy.

If you are looking for a pet, ask the breeder why the puppy is designated pet quality. Take this element into account when evaluating the overall dog. The fault may be a flowered tongue, large ears, narrow muzzle, coat color deviating from the standard, etc. Puppies with flowered or spotted tongues are often very attractive and can make wonderful companions.

Above all, pet or show, you want a dog that is both physically and emotionally sound. A shy or aggressive puppy is not sound. While they may remain aloof with strangers, Shar-Pei do not usually react strongly to a new environment or activity.

You will find that Chinese Shar-Pei puppies will walk into your home and take over as if they've been there all their lives. A firm hand and some discipline will determine whether you own a Shar-Pei or he owns you. Don't let the cuteness get to you; all puppies test their limits. What may be cute in a puppy could be disastrous in an adult dog, however. Remember, the Chinese Shar-Pei is a thinking breed and has to be taught good judgment.

All puppies need to extend their experience beyond basic bodily needs. A dog that is always kept in the house may be a good companion, but he will usually develop behavior problems when taken out into the world because he doesn't know any better. Puppy socialization is the key to good behavior and later training.

Puppies learning the ups and downs of stairs. Owner: Helen Armacost.

Three puppies from
the World of Wrinkles.
Owned by Linda and
Mike Schatzburg.
Crezentia

Ben Chings Dizzie at eight months of age.
Owner: J. Gardner.   *V. Kelly*

Ben Chings Nan Hai v Ming Yu, owned b
Linda Teitelbaum.   *V. Kel*

The puppy should remain in the home until he has had all his shots. No puppy should be taken to a dog show prior to three months of age. It is simply too dangerous. There are too many viruses to which a young puppy is highly susceptible when not fully immunized.

Early lessons on discipline should begin as soon as he becomes a member of your home. Even though he may already be housebroken, he needs to adapt to your schedule. Be consistent and praise good behavior. Your puppy is building confidence and becoming secure with his new family. If there are other dogs and children, supervise the interaction with the puppy. While other dogs or children should not be rough with a puppy, neither should the puppy terrorize the other household members.

Interaction with humans is especially important between eight and twelve weeks of age. This establishes the bond between animal and man. Discipline is also necessary, but should be gentle. The dog is capable of learning basic commands and acceptable behavior. You are earning the respect of your new canine companion.

Having a puppy at this age is equivalent to having an active toddler in the house. Chinese Shar-Pei are curious. They will be into everything and need constant supervision. If the puppy is not already crate trained, start now. Crating is not cruel. It provides the puppy with a secure environment and makes your life much easier. Crating also protects the puppy from household hazards while you are occupied elsewhere. It is safer when traveling to keep the dog in a crate rather than have him loose in the car, which allows him to get under foot or to be thrown about in the event of an accident.

Begin by crating the puppy a few minutes several times a day. Provide him with toys or a bone (no food or water). Eventually you will find that he enjoys his new home and will often go inside the crate to sleep or for some quiet time away from day-to-day activities.

From three to four months of age the puppy needs outside experience. He should be out meeting new people and developing his public demeanor. He has to learn what is expected of him in each situation. He will be cutting teeth. Vigilance will keep house and furniture intact. Whenever the pup starts to chew, present him with a nylon bone and tell him, "Take." In this way the puppy learns a command and you can praise him instead of scolding him. This has proven an easy and effective way to survive the chewing phase.

Kindergarten puppy training is excellent. This is a program of basic obedience training coupled with exercises to establish and strengthen your relationship with the dog. Most local dog clubs or obedience training schools offer this "basic training" course for owners and puppies and it is

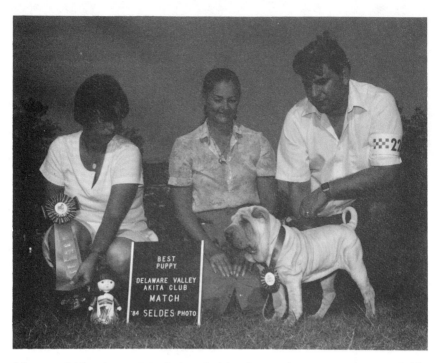

Scirrocco of Masada, owned and handled by Blaine Miles.   *Seldes*

Seven-week-old puppies at DJ's Shar-Pei. Owner: Debra and John Corr.

especially valuable for novice owners. As the puppy tries to establish dominance over you, training is mandatory. Chinese Shar-Pei like to be dominant.

Upon reaching four months, your Shar-Pei is an adolescent. Chinese Shar-Pei grow quite rapidly. The body matures before the dog has the mental or emotional capacity to deal with all situations. This is often described as being the "out to lunch" period and you must remember he is still young and impressionable. He will be more independent, test his limits and venture out on his own. A firm hand is required to mold acceptable behavior.

As the Shar-Pei matures into adolescence, hormonal changes will affect personality. At some point males will discover the lure of females. His behavior will be dictated by his raging hormones. While some Shar-Pei are more determined than others, it will be difficult to keep his attention on you. He will be gaping around at everything. A firm hand in making him behave may not always be successful, but you must keep trying to get his attention. Be gentle and consistent in discipline. This is a difficult period that all Shar-Pei go through. An understanding owner will bring him through to a more responsible adulthood.

There will be lucid moments when the veil lifts and the adult dog appears. They will be brief at first. A Shar-Pei can take up to two years to mature mentally and emotionally.

While the mind struggles to catch up with the body, there will also be subtle physical changes. You won't notice the changes because you see him everyday. However, they will be obvious to visitors and his breeder. The body becomes heavier, the chest drops down to its proper position and the musculature builds and increases the bulk of the dog.

It can take up to three years for a Chinese Shar-Pei to come into his own, depending upon the line. Males are usually slower than females. Male puppies are slower starters and are subject to more ills. Female puppies are stronger and pull themselves together earlier; although females go through the same stages, they move through them more quickly. A female can be ready to take on the world by two years of age, while a male is still fumbling around.

The males tend to be slower and more laid back in every way. If you are going to have a problem with owning multiple Shar-Pei, it will be the females who start the trouble, not the males.

Is it worth the work? Yes. An adult Shar-Pei is a devoted companion. He can help you make friends, melt the hardest heart and provide hours of entertainment.

Multiple Shar-Pei live together peacefully at Krim Sun Shar-Pei, Long Island, New York, with owners Maureen and Richard Scuteri.

8
Care of the Chinese Shar-Pei

IT HAS BEEN SAID that the Chinese Shar-Pei is a veterinarian's nightmare. Although some of the early dogs had multiple health problems, the Shar-Pei is not necessarily subject to more ills than other dogs.

As a rare breed, the Chinese Shar-Pei does not have the history of most other breeds. Many veterinarians are unfamiliar with the Shar-Pei's problems and requirements. We are still learning about these dogs. Your veterinarian must be willing to listen to you and openmindedly discuss problems. A positive attitude and open communication is essential for a successful relationship between you and your veterinarian.

If you already have a veterinarian, ask him or her about their feelings for Chinese Shar-Pei. If this is your first animal, ask your breeder or other local Shar-Pei owners who their veterinarian is and if they are happy with the care their dog receives.

On your first visit, shortly after the puppy comes homes, watch how the dog reacts to the veterinarian. Can you, the dog and the veterinarian establish a good rapport? If not, try someone else.

Although one veterinarian can take care of most of your dog's requirements, realize that there are specialties within veterinary medicine. If the puppy has entropion, it is better to consult a veterinary ophthalmologist rather than someone attempting their first entropion surgery. There are breeding specialists, orthopedic specialists, and many others. Your primary veterinarian can refer you to specialists in your community or nearby.

The Chinese Shar-Pei is subject to the ailments of any breed. Explanations for conditions affecting dogs are available in many good medical books written for the dog owner. Problems of which every Shar-Pei owner should be aware are explained below. This does not mean your puppy will be affected, but you will be prepared should a problem arise.

Many, if not all, of the medical conditions described below are hereditary. With the exception of the eye problems, which appear in the majority of the breed, you should think hard before breeding dogs that display genetic defects. Do you want to promote these qualities in the Chinese Shar-Pei? Eliminating faulty dogs from breeding programs is the first step in eliminating these conditions in future generations.

EYES

Entropion. In this condition the eyelids roll inward, causing the lashes to irritate the cornea. The constant rubbing can cause corneal abrasions and eventually ulceration. If the condition is left untreated, the ulcer could perforate, leading to blindness.

The preferred treatment, according to Dr. James Clinton of the Animal Eye Clinic in New Jersey, is entropion surgery. Dr. Clinton is a diplomate of the American College of Veterinary Ophthalmologists and regularly performs corrective surgery on Chinese Shar-Pei.

He estimates that over 95 percent of Shar-Pei would benefit from some type of entropion correction. "Eyes and lids that don't fit properly are not a sign of poor quality, they are just part of the breed," says Dr. Clinton.

Entropion can occur before the puppies open their eyes, though this is rare. Usually between two weeks of age, when the eyes open, and fourteen months of age, the dog will exhibit signs of mild to severe entropion. It is the owner's responsibility to check the eyes daily for any unusual discharge. Puppies will often indicate a problem by pawing at their eyes or faces. Until you can reach a veterinarian, lubricate the eyes with artificial tear products such as Lacrilube or Duratears. These are available in drug stores without a prescription. Never use eyedrops containing steroids. Take the dog to a veterinarian as soon as possible.

When the condition develops in puppies under 17 weeks of age, many veterinarians prefer tacking to surgery. Tacking involves suturing the eyelid away from the eye. However, tacking can cause scarring and may have to be repeated. Later, surgery is sometimes necessary to correct the results of tacking as well as to correct the entropion.

Dr. Clinton believes that entropion surgery is the answer to correcting the Shar-Pei eye problems. Through careful use of anesthesia, the procedure can be done on any puppy more than 20 days old. The affected

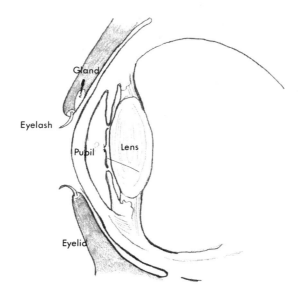

1. Normal Eyelids

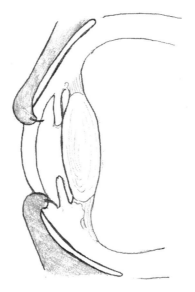

2. Eyelids with Entropion Lids turned in, lashes touching cornea surface.

121

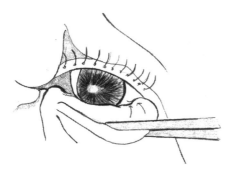

Affected eyelid is everted to correct position.

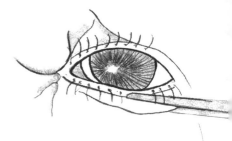

A piece of skin with underlying muscle tissue removed in an eliptical section.

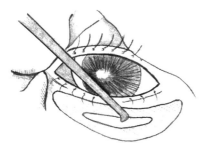

The open incision is to the eyelid margin.

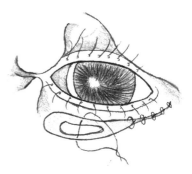

Sutured incision.

Entropion surgery is often performed to correct the problem and return the eyelids to normal position.

eyelid is everted and an elliptical section of skin and the underlying muscle are removed. The correctly aligned eyelid is then sutured. In this way the problem is permanently corrected. The eyes look great and scarring is not evident.

Ectropion. Some dogs suffer the opposite problem. Rather than rolling in, the eyelid rolls away from the eye. This exposes the eye to irritation from the environment. Again, artificial tears will help until you can get the dog to a veterinarian.

Dr. Clinton has seen dogs with entropion and ectropion in the same eye. He says that if the entropion is corrected, the ectropion usually improves. Ectropion, unless severe, is usually a cosmetic rather than a health problem.

Cherry Eye. With cherry eye, the gland situated in the third eyelid becomes inflamed. The small muscle-like fibers that surround it are not strong enough to hold the swollen gland in place. It appears at the inside corner of the eye as a bright pink or reddish swelling. This is not uncommon in Shar-Pei.

Eye ointments may or may not resolve the problem. If surgery is required, suturing the gland back to the nicotens or third eyelid is preferred over more extensive surgery. This gland is instrumental in providing tears to lubricate the eye, and total amputation of the gland is not recommended.

An alternative procedure is to amputate one-half of the gland and suture the remainder to the nicotens, in which case one must wait to see if the gland will retain some function.

Dry Eye. This condition results from insufficient tear production. The eye is not properly lubricated and ulceration can occur. Artificial tears can provide some relief until the tears return or surgery is performed. Dry eye can be a side effect of complete amputation of the gland affected in cherry eye.

EARS

Chinese Shar-Pei have tiny ear canals. Their folded ears prevent air from circulating in the ear, so bacteria can build up and ear infections can become chronic.

It is important to check the ears daily and to keep the canal meticulously clean. If you smell any odor coming from the ear, consult your veterinarian. The quicker the problem is treated, the less likely it will become chronic.

Tacking is another procedure used to correct entropion.

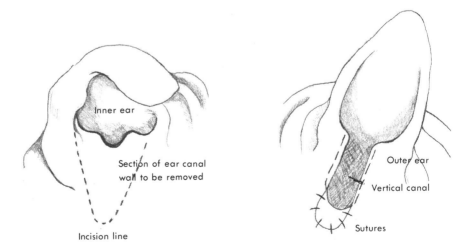

Inner ear

Section of ear canal
wall to be removed

Incision line

Outer ear

Vertical canal

Sutures

The Shar-Pei have small ear canals that may be prone to infection. In severe cases an ear resection will solve the problem.

In severe cases an ear resection may be necessary to expose the ear canal. In this procedure the outer ear wall is removed to allow air to circulate, thereby keeping the ear canal dry.

MOUTH

Tight Lip. In this condition, the lower lip rolls up and over the lower teeth. The lip is very tight and almost impossible to roll downward to expose the bite. This condition is uncomfortable for the dog and can also exert pressure on the lower teeth and push them back. The mouth becomes overshot, with the upper teeth protruding over the lower. This can lead to eating difficulties. Surgery is needed to relieve the problem.

Elongated Soft Palate. This is a major cause of snoring and most Shar-Pei probably have it to a degree. If the puppy does not have problems breathing, eating or does not tire easily, don't worry. If he does show signs of these problems, consult your veterinarian to see if surgery is required.

NOSE

Stenotic Noses. In this condition the nostrils are compressed when the puppy inhales. This closes the air passage. Surgery corrects the problem by removing part of the nose or nostrils to facilitate breathing.

SKIN

Dermatitis. Dermatitis, a catch-all term for skin inflammation, can be caused by allergies, hypothyroidism or parasites. Some skin problems are outgrown; others become chronic. In Shar-Pei the incidence of dermatitis is greater in the horse or short coats than in the longer brush coats. Many early Shar-Pei suffered from severe skin problems. Today, the incidence is much lower and your dog may never be affected. Should a dog have severe skin problems, he should never be bred.

Demodectic Mange. This condition is also known as *red mange*, and is the most common form of mange. It is caused by a parasitic mite that thrives in the hair follicles. All dogs have mites, but most dogs are resistant to these parasites. The inability to resist these mites is an inherited characteristic. The first signs of demodectic mange are small hairless patches. As the condition progresses, patches of skin will redden and may become scaly, with some areas developing into open sores.

Mild cases of demodectic mange may reverse themselves as the dog's natural immunity builds up or after treatment. Generalized democodosis can further depress the dog's immune system and set up a vicious cycle of illness.

ALLERGIES

A continuing cause of skin problems, allergies are common in all dogs, including Shar-Pei. An allergy to flea bites is, perhaps, the most common allergy problem. Whenever a flea bites, it releases a toxin into the dog's system. The main symptom of an allergic reaction is generalized scratching, causing hot spots. Hot spots are infections under the skin that the dog can open by licking. These patches will be hairless and moist. Your veterinarian can recommend a topical product to dry out hot spots and relieve skin irritation. The best cure is a flealess environment, as it takes only one bite to affect a flea-sensitive dog.

Many skin conditions are a mystery to both Shar-Pei owners and veterinarians. These are probably caused by undiscovered allergies. Broad spectrum antibodies rarely work and should be used only as a last resort. Surprisingly, hemorrhoid ointment has resolved some of the mystery ailments such as hairless ears. This product contains an antiinflammatory agent, as well as zinc, which has been known to encourage hair growth. Remember, however, to discuss the situation with your veterinarian before trying *any* home remedies.

INTERNAL PROBLEMS

Megaesophagus. In this condition the esophagus is dilated, causing food and water to divert from the pathway of the throat to the stomach. The most common symptom is regurgitation of food. The condition can usually be detected at weaning or shortly thereafter. Slow weight gain, coupled with regurgitation, indicate megaesophagus. The degree of dilation of the esophagus varies. In severe cases aspiration-pneumonia may result and the prognosis for recovery is poor.

Immune Deficiency. This condition follows certain Shar-Pei lines. The puppy may spike a high fever for no apparent reason. The depressed immune system does not properly respond to infectious agents and susceptibility to demodectic mange. The more depressed the system, the greater the problems.

In some cases, the dog's immune system will pick up by itself. Where the immune system is severely depressed or further depressed by health problems, the cycle may become chronic.

126

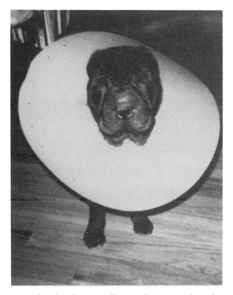

An Elizabethan Collar will keep the dog
from scratching the affected area.

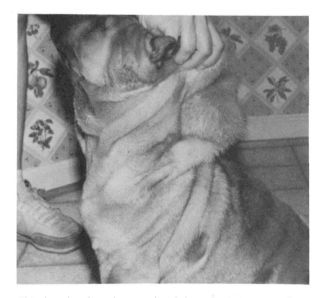

This dog developed generalized demodectic mange at four
months of age.

Thyroid. Hypothyroidism or low thyroid output has shown up in some Chinese Shar-Pei. This is the most common endocrine problem in dogs. The symptoms usually appear between two to five years of age and include lethargy, lack of endurance, sparse and dry coats, skin problems, thickening and darkening of the skin and breeding problems. A blood test can determine the concentration of thyroid hormones in the dog's system. Treatment is available and is usually successful in reversing the symptoms in most dogs.

STRUCTURAL CONDITIONS

Hip Dysplasia. In dogs suffering from hip dysplasia (HD) the hip socket or the head of the femur is improperly formed, allowing excessive movement in the joint. Continuous pressure results in calcium deposits, inflammation and arthritis. Cases range from mild to severe. Severe dysplasia is a painful and crippling condition. Diagnosis is by x-ray.

The OFA, Orthopedic Foundation for Animals, has a system for evaluating x-rays and grading hips from exellent through severely dysplastic. Although the condition can appear at an early age, the OFA requires that the animal be at least two years of age before they will assign a permanent number that attests that the dog is free of HD. The organization will evaluate x-rays prior to two years and render an opinion, but this is only a preliminary opinion and a new set of x-rays will have to be taken after two years of age.

Patella luxation. Whether inherited or due to an injury, patella luxation is a condition in which the patella or kneecap slips out of place. Normally, the patella is held in place by muscle and tissues. If this support structure is weakened, the patella can move. This condition is also known as slipped stifles.

CORTISONE DRUGS AS TREATMENT

Chinese Shar-Pei are often given cortisone-based drugs for various ills. One side effect particular to the Shar-Pei is that they "lose their muzzle." You can almost see it melt away. The padding on the muzzle has a great deal of water in the tissue. As the cortisone reduces the water content, the muzzle reduces in size. The degree of reduction depends on whether the size of the muzzle is based on bone or mostly padding. Once use of the drug is discontinued, the muzzle slowly returns to its former fullness.

SHAR-PEI SYNDROME

George H. Muller, D.V.M., described a condition called *Shar-Pei Syndrome* in the November 1986 issue of the *Barker*.

The dog's skin becomes red and inflamed. Hair loss is mostly on the underside of the dog, though some exhibit hair loss over the whole body. When the loss occurs in patches, the dog looks moth eaten.

The significant factor is that all tests to locate the problem are negative. The cause is unknown and the symptoms respond poorly to treatment.

This may be the dog's equivalent of Shar-Pei rash. The dog may be reacting to the prickly hair irritating his *own* skin.

9
Grooming

THE CHINESE SHAR-PEI is left entirely natural. No trimming is required or allowed.

COAT

The coat is short and coarse. It tends to repel dirt and should not smell "doggy" even when wet. The Shar-Pei sheds little throughout the year. The most noticeable shedding occurs after a bitch weans her puppies. Thus, the Shar-Pei does not require frequent brushing. Since the coat does not mat, a quick going over with a good bristle brush or grooming mitt will keep the coat clean and healthy. The key to a healthy coat is good nutrition, not the amount of grooming performed.

Shar-Pei do not usually develop an offensive odor unless there is a problem. Hence, frequent bathing is unnecessary. Light-colored dogs may require a bath before a show, whereas the darker dogs can usually do with a light clean up. Wet a towel and run it over the top of the coat to remove dirt. The natural coarseness of the hair repels most grime, which is easily removed.

Frequent bathing can remove the natural oils present in the coat and skin, leading to a form of dandruff. During the occasional shampoo do not use cream rinse. Cream rinse softens the coat, and the Shar-Pei coat is supposed to be coarse. There is no reason to cream rinse a dog that has a coat that does not tangle or mat. Leave the complicated grooming to those with the long-coated breeds; caring for the Chinese Shar-Pei should be easy.

The only problem you may have with grooming the Shar-Pei is getting him to agree to a bath. Shar-Pei hate water. Start with the young puppy and get him used to the procedure early. He will probably always resent a bath, but he won't object too strenuously.

EARS

Make it a weekly habit to check your Shar-Pei's ears. They are prone to ear infections. If there is a smell coming from the ear canal, consult your veterinarian. Clean away any deposits with a piece of cotton moistened with a little warm water. There are some excellent ear cleaning products on the market that make this task even easier.

Chinese Shar-Pei are also subject to ear mite infestation. Black dirt in the ear canal signals a problem, which can be readily cleared up using medication available from your veterinarian.

You should also be very careful when bathing the dog not to allow water to enter the ears.

NAILS

Again, accustom your dog to having his nails cut by starting early. As soon as the puppy comes home begin the procedure. Chinese Shar-Pei loathe having their feet touched. However, they can be trained to tolerate the procedure if you handle it properly.

Shar-Pei should have tight feet. Nails must be kept short to prevent splaying of the feet.

Be especially careful with dark nails. The vein extends almost to the end of the nail and takes longer to recede in Shar-Pei than in other breeds. Removing a sliver of the nail every third or fourth day will slowly allow the vein to recede. It takes time to shorten Shar-Pei nails, but it can be done.

Light nails are easier to cut. Hold the nail sideways up to a light. You can see where the vein ends; therefore, you should be able to avoid cutting it.

Should you accidently cut into a vein, there are several products available to stop the bleeding. If nothing else is available, household flour will do the trick. No dog has ever died from a bleeding nail, but a dog will begin to shy away from manicures if you cut the vein too often. It hurts!

TEETH

Allow the dog plenty of nylon bones and hard biscuits, which aid in keeping teeth clean. Owners can scale the dog's teeth at home, but due to the structure of the Chinese Shar-Pei mouth this is difficult. When scaling becomes necessary, take the dog to your veterinarian.

GROOMING FOR THE SHOW RING

Good grooming for the Chinese Shar-Pei is the same for pet and show dogs. For the show ring, the Shar-Pei should be clean and healthy. Dirty dogs are an affront to the judge.

No trimming of the coat is necessary or allowed. The Shar-Pei do not grow excessive hair between the pads nor on the rear pasterns. The whiskers are left on the dog's muzzle.

Most of the work preparing to show a Chinese Shar-Pei involves checking problem areas. Are the ears clean? Does the dog have an ear infection? Is there any discharge from the eyes? Are the eyes bright and clear? Are the nails short so that the feet are tight? Is the skin and coat clean and healthy? Are the teeth clean? Is the coat intact or has the dog been chewing at himself, indicating a problem? Dogs with any problem, health or otherwise, should not be shown.

10

Breeding and
Puppy Rearing

$\mathbf{Y}$OUR BREEDING PROGRAM starts with the foundation bitch. She should be the best you can buy.

If you are limited in the number of dogs you can have, but want to breed, buy females rather than males. You can always pay a stud fee for use of a male. This gives you an unlimited source of stud dogs. Even if you have a male on the premises, you will still want to go outside for breeding on occasion. Using the same male for every breeding limits your program.

Becoming a good breeder is hard work. The whole point of breeding is to move closer and closer to the ideal dog as described in the written standard. You must understand genetics, research the characteristics behind your foundation stock, decide what is good and bad with your own dog, and so on. Be honest in your evaluations. It is better to be too picky than to be kennel blind.

The Chinese Shar-Pei is a new breed in the United States. It may be impossible to trace the ancestry of your dog prior to 1976, if even back that far. Dogs today usually have a complete three-generation pedigree, and some dogs can be traced back seven or more generations. Go as far back as you can.

Most Chinese Shar-Pei imports were the result of linebreeding. Linebreeding involves the mating of a dog and a bitch who have one or more relatives in common. Linebred dogs are not as closely related as those produced by inbreeding, which is the mating of dogs from within close family lines. Inbreeding is used to "fix" positive features coming from both sides of the pedigree.

Ch. Bruce Lee's Cierra ML of Viv one day before whelping. Owner: Vivien Kelly.

Ch. Cinderella Joss and her two-and-a-half-week-old puppies. Breeder: Kandi Stirling.

In most cases novice breeders should follow a plan of linebreeding. It is difficult to find an outcross — a totally unrelated dog — because most of the original Shar-Pei in the United States came from one kennel and have common ancestors.

There are many excellent books on the art of breeding. These books explain the basics of genetics, the process of breeding, whelping, etc. Read several books and consult with an experienced breeder before embarking on breeding your Shar-Pei. In this chapter we will deal with items particular to the Chinese Shar-Pei as a breed.

A BACKGROUND ON BREEDING SHAR-PEI

The Chinese Shar-Pei bitch comes into season twice a year, about every six months. Her first heat will usually be between six and ten months of age.

A bitch must be mature both physically and mentally before she is bred. While she may appear physically mature at one year, she is not ready to be bred. Sixteen to eighteen months of age is a more reasonable time for a first mating. However, not all Shar-Pei are ready at that age. Don't force the issue. Your bitch may be telling you she's not ready yet. If she doesn't want to be bred, don't make her accept the male. It is better to wait another six months.

Any Shar-Pei that is to be used in a breeding program should be x-rayed and pronounced clear of hip dysplasia prior to mating. If the dog is under two years of age, the hips can receive preliminary approval. At 18 months of age there is a strong probability that the dog will pass at two years if the preliminary evaluation is excellent or good. A dog rated fair should not be bred until the final decision on the hips is made at two years. Any dog over two years of age can have the x-rays of the hips evaluated and receive a permanent number from the OFA if the dog is determined to be free of hip dysplasia. Only dogs that have been shown to be clear of hip dysplasia should be used for breeding.

The short coat of the Shar-Pei makes it easy to spot the start of a season. The average bitch will accept a male between the tenth and eighteenth day — but don't count on your bitch being average. Some have bred as early as the fifth day while others have waited until the twenty-sixth day.

MATING

The Shar-Pei male is ritualistic when it comes to the breeding process. Before mounting the bitch your male will dance and sing. He will posture for the bitch and invite her to play.

The biggest problem may be the bitch. Many Shar-Pei bitches are dominant and do not take kindly to males putting their paws on her back. Some experienced studs have developed a way to mount a bitch without offending her sensibilities. If not, the owner should hold the bitch, calming her down and distracting her attention from the male. If the owner is not available and the bitch is still recalcitrant, a muzzle may work. If she still refuses the male, reevaluate if she is ready for the breeding or if she may have a physical problem.

Shar-Pei have tested low for thyroid hormones. A low thyroid output will make the bitch reluctant about breeding. Even when a hypothyroid is bred, she will often not conceive.

If all else fails and you determine you still want the bitch bred, consider artificial insemination. This procedure may only be done by a licensed veterinarian if you want to register the litter. The Chinese Shar-Pei Club of America provides for the registration of litters by artificial insemination using fresh semen, fresh extended semen and frozen semen. The following article details the CSPCA requirements.

Artificial Insemination Using Fresh Semen

The CSPCA will consider an application to register a litter resulting from artificial insemination provided both the sire and dam are present during the artificial mating, and provided that both the extraction and insemination are done by the same licensed veterinarian.

A certificate on a form provided by the CSPCA must be completed by the person(s) who owned the sire and dam (or lessee, if dam was leased) on the date of mating. (If the dam was leased at the time of mating, the lessee must file a "Report of Lease of Bitch/Dog" form with CSPCA.)

A certificate form is also required of the licensed veterinarian who effected the artificial breeding.

Before submitting a litter application to record a litter produced by artificial insemination, it is essential that the "Certificate of Breeding by Artificial Insemination" form be completed so that it can be attached to the litter application when the application is mailed to the CSPCA.

Using Fresh Extended Semen

The Chinese Shar-Pei Club of America, Inc. will consider an application to register a litter resulting from artificial insemination of the bitch using fresh extended semen provided the semen is extracted and extended by a licensed veterinarian, the insemination of the bitch is performed by a licensed veterinarian and the litter is eligible for registration in all other respects. The semen must be extracted from males within *the USA* and shipped to points within *the USA only*.

Same sire, different dams. In the center is Ch. Gung Ho's Eminent Domain. To the left is MP Gung Ho's Blue Jasper and to the right is MP Gung Ho's Ping Ki Li. All are owned by Peg Kastner of Eminent Kennels. *Bob Barber*

Ch. Panda and her nine puppies at four days of age. Breeder: Maryann Smithers.

Gung Ho's Hot Shot of TOP, owned by Gerald Griffin, contemplating a toy.

The certification on a form provided by CSPCA must be completed and submitted with a litter registration application form and litter registration fee. If the dam was leased at the time of mating, the lessee must file a "Report of Lease of Bitch/Dog" form and fee with the CSPCA.

Using Frozen Semen

The CSPCA will consider an application (on a form provided by CSPCA) to register a litter resulting from artificial insemination using frozen semen, provided the litter is, in all respects, eligible for registration and the following conditions are met.

1. The Collection of semen for the artificial breeding must have been reported to the CSPCA, and the collector/storer must be on record with the CSPCA as familiar with and complying with CSPCA regulations for record keeping and identification of dogs.

It is further stated that

1. It is the intention of CSPCA to follow the current procedure of AKC.

2. The certifications on a form provided by CSPCA must be completed by the owner of the semen, the owner of the dam and the veterinarian who performed the artificial breeding.

PREGNANCY

A Shar-Pei bitch in whelp is very amiable. She becomes extremely affectionate and loves your attention. However, other bitches in the house may resent her. Be careful when they are together and divide your attentions accordingly.

Shar-Pei gain weight all over when in whelp. The bitch will look "well upholstered." It is often hard to tell if she is pregnant or simply overweight. Toward the last two weeks, her pregnancy will be easier to discern as she starts to bulge and has trouble getting around.

Shar-Pei usually whelp earlier than the average 63-day canine gestation period, so be prepared for whelping from day 56 on. Shar-Pei give plenty of warning when they go into labor. The bitch will appear agitated, refusing to lie in one place for any length of time. She will pant excessively. You can expect puppies eight to 12 hours later.

Don't be surprised if you don't notice that her water has broken. Many Shar-Pei create only a small wet spot, which could just as easily have come from her salivating while panting or cleaning herself.

The bitch must be attended while whelping. You may not have to do anything, but emergencies are always possible. The bitch may not break the sac. The puppy may be lethargic and need help to get going. Any number of situations may occur calling for your intervention.

Shar-Pei generally make good mothers. They are often reluctant to leave their puppies and will have to be forced outside to relieve themselves.

The number of puppies in a Shar-Pei litter can vary from one to ten. The average is three to five. The bitch will usually tell you when she's done. She'll stretch out, look relaxed and allow her brood to suckle. She may even tell you to get lost by emitting a low rumble or giving a light nip. She wants to be alone with her babies. Humor her.

SHAR-PEI NEWBORNS

Shar-Pei puppies look like most other puppies. They may have few or no wrinkles, but the distinctive nose is evident.

Wrinkles begin to appear around two to three weeks of age and continue to develop until three or four months. At that time they begn to disappear again, as an adult dog retains only a moderate amount of wrinkling on the head and shoulders.

You can usually determine basic coat length — horse or brush — at birth. Determining variations in length between the two main coats will have to wait.

Color is not easily determined. The blacks and creams are the easiest to spot. Creams are born white. When a white puppy appears, check the ears, nose, mouth and pads of feet for pigmentation. The presence of any pigment rules out albinoism, a breed disqualification. White puppies darken quickly and you will soon know that it is cream. The typical cream can be an off-white to a light color. Their ears have a distinctive apricot hue.

The other colors are more difficult to evaluate at birth. Puppies are born in varying shades of brown and may appear striped or mottled. The flowered or spotted puppy is easy to pick out and should not be confused with a solid-colored dog with darker shading or mottling.

Colors will lighten or darken as the puppies grow. Even at eight weeks of age a fawn may still become a red, or vice versa. After six months the color will not change.

Shar-Pei pigmentation starts to appear as early as one week of age. Remember, all Shar-Pei are born with pink tongues. Some will have a dot of pigment on the tongue or a small smudge on the nose. These dogs usually have the darkest pigment, which fills in earlier than on other dogs. Nevertheless, all puppies have an equal chance at birth of becoming fully pigmented. The filling in of the pigment can take as little as three weeks or

140

Xanadu Chi, owned by Barbara Wainer.

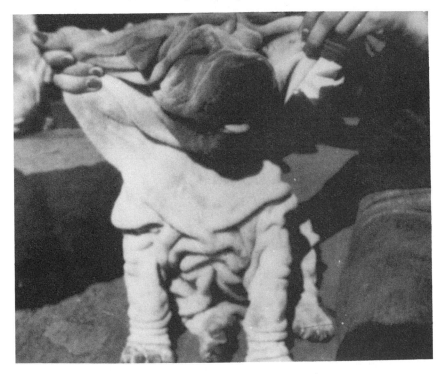

A size six Fingertail puppy in a size twelve suit.

141

A strong stud dog will
be unmistakably
masculine.

Bonnie modeling her denim britches.

142

as long as three to four months. Small pink spots in a young puppy have a good chance of filling in later. A predominantly pink tongue at eight weeks probably will not change.

The newborn Shar-Pei has a straight tail. The tail won't begin to come up until about three weeks of age, and may take much longer to curl. An eight-week-old puppy should carry his tail over his back. The final amount of curl will come with maturity.

The eyes open at around two weeks of age. Check the eyes daily for signs of entropion, tearing and/or pawing at the eyes. Though it is rare for entropion to occur before the eyes open, it has happened. If a puppy has not opened his eyes by three weeks of age, have him checked by a veterinary ophthalmologist.

Shar-Pei sometimes have a condition referred to as "hidden eye." Shar-Pei eyes are deeply set and occasionally the eye is not visible when the eyelids open. Usually only one eye is affected. The eye usually surfaces by three months, but may be more deeply recessed than the one that was not as deeply set.

Shar-Pei snort and snore even as small puppies. This is normal, but be aware of conditions such as stenotic noses, tight lip and elongated soft palate, which can all cause serious problems.

Weaning puppies is always messy — half the food ends up in the puppy and the other half is smeared across the face. Carefully clean off Shar-Pei faces after feeding, as food may become lodged in the wrinkling and cause irritation.

Some Shar-Pei need encouragement to eat solid food. Shar-Pei are clean animals and may not want to get their faces dirty. Some dogs have solved the problem by eating out of the opposite side of the bowl so that their upper lip rests on the rim.

Enjoy the puppies while they are young. When they play and romp, you'll notice their personalities emerging. You may start picking out the show and pet puppies, but wait to make the final decision until eight or nine weeks of age. Puppies change constantly and can really surprise you.

Handle the puppies daily so that they get used to human contact. Never let a puppy go to a new home before seven or eight weeks of age. The time spent with the dam and littermates is too important to his future development.

Mother and son take Best of Breed and Best of Opposite Sex at the Culpepper Kennel Club under judge Ingrid Strasser. Ch. Bruce Lee's Bonnie Brenna is BOB and Ch. Gung Ho's Captain Jiggs is BOS. Both are owned by Alice Lawler. *Bruce Harkins*

The cultured gentle-
man always comes
in first.

11

Showing the Chinese Shar-Pei

DOG SHOWING IS A SPORT. Many people find the competition exhilarating. Others think *dog people* are crazy. Dog showing is also hard work. Training, grooming and traveling take substantial time and resources. However, dog showing is also fun for the many dog show enthusiasts.

If your puppy is show quality — a very good to excellent example of the Chinese Shar-Pei — you should give the show world a chance. It is a good way to meet other owners and breeders, exchange information and generally have a good time. If your plans include breeding, you should plan on showing your dog.

Conformation shows are designed to judge how closely your dog conforms to the breed's written standard. Though each show provides only one opinion, every evaluation is important. There are always people on the show grounds willing to look at and evaluate your dog. You will learn what is good and bad in the breed, see other dogs and learn to evaluate structure and movement as it typifies the Chinese Shar-Pei. You may even win a ribbon or two!

TRAINING

Conformation showing is not a beauty contest. The dogs are evaluated along specific guidelines. Your dog will be expected to move in certain patterns, stand for examination and exhibit a calm, even temperament.

145

Khan-Du winners, owned by Elly Paulus.

Best of Breed is Ch. Bruce Lee's Ting of Ripple, owned by Rose Ellen and Morgan Stone. The dog on the left is Best of Opposite Sex Ch. Bruce Lee's Keisha Deberic, also owned by the Stones. The judge is Elly Paulus.   *Bob Barber*

Ch. Blue Nun, owned by Kandi Stirling.

Ch. Bruce Lee's Kai Tug Lee, owned by Elly
Paulus.   *Bruce Harkins*

Ch. Hillie's Roisin Rua-Gung Ho, owned by
Alice Lawler.   *Bruce Harkins*

Training for conformation is as specific as training for obedience. The dog learns what performance is expected by repetition.

The Chinese Shar-Pei puppy destined for the show ring should begin training early. Shar-Pei do not like having their feet touched or their mouths opened, and both these procedures will have to be done during judging in the conformation ring.

Most dogs will need to be stacked (to have their legs and feet placed properly). This involves your picking up the leg and placing each foot in its proper position. Daily practice of the procedure will make life easier on you and your dog.

The judge will examine the bite and mouth or ask that you, as handler, show the bite and mouth. Showing the mouth is difficult in many Shar-Pei. The abundant padding of the muzzle is sometimes hard to pull back from the teeth. The fact that Shar-Pei slobber also makes the lips hard to handle. Inexperienced dogs quickly get tired of the fussing required to show the bite and mouth. Starting early with the puppy will make the process easier.

Gently pull the lips back, top and bottom, until the teeth are exposed. With heavy-headed dogs, you may have to hook a finger inside the lip to pull it back. Then insert your finger on the side of the mouth to part the teeth and show the tongue. Practice will make showing the bite and mouth a quick and easy procedure.

To learn the patterns and finer points of handling, attend local handling classes. Handling classes involve groups of dogs in a pseudo ring situation. Besides training both you and the dog, the classes aid the socialization needed for all show dogs. Many experienced handlers take puppies to handling classes for the exposure.

WHERE TO SHOW

The Chinese Shar-Pei is a rare breed and not eligible to enter American Kennel Club point shows or sanctioned matches. However, there are many nonaffiliated clubs sponsoring fun matches with rare breeds invited. Though these matches are informal events for AKC-recognized breeds, they can be sanctioned point shows for the Chinese Shar-Pei.

The Chinese Shar-Pei Club of America (CSPCA) will not recognize or record points earned toward championship titles unles they are acquired at a show that has been previously approved or sanctioned. Sanctioning requires that an application for show approval be submitted to the CSPCA at least 90 days in advance for a specialty and at least 45 days before other shows.

A specialty is hosted by local affiliated Chinese Shar-Pei clubs and only Chinese Shar-Pei can compete. No other breed is eligible to enter.

Ch. Genaul Megan Xanadu, CD, owned by Helen Armacost.

Ch. Shooting Star, owned by Kandi Stirling.

Junior Handler Tigger Stirling with Pat.

Junior handler Trevor Stirling with
Ch. Canon Copier.

Sanctioned shows may be for Chinese Shar-Pei only and hosted by an affiliated club or may be hosted by a nonaffiliated club with other breeds being shown.

Sanctioning serves several purposes. It gives the CSPCA control over which shows are point shows. It assures exhibitors that there won't be multiple point shows in one given area on the same day. It also means that point shows are sponsored by valid clubs, with knowledgeable judges. Cheap championships earned at backyard shows do the breed no good. The title champion should have meaning. Sanctioning assures the title continued respect.

Applications for sanctioning are submitted by the host club. Forms are available from the CSPCA or a local affiliated club. Listings of Chinese Shar-Pei sanctioned shows are available from the Chinese Shar-Pei Club of America. Rare breed shows are listed in the *Match Show Bulletin*, which is available by subscription from Grace Sachs, Box 214, Massapequa, NY 11758. Check to make sure the show has been approved before attending. If the show is not sanctioned, you can still show for fun and practice, but not points.

WHO MAY ENTER

Anyone in good standing with the Chinese Shar-Pei Club of America and the American Kennel Club may enter a show. Dogs over six months of age show for points. Most clubs provide classes for younger puppies, but these are fun classes for practice and carry no point awards.

In order to earn points toward a championship title, your dog must be registered with the CSPCA within 30 days after his first show and you must be a member of the CSPCA.

You will not be required to present your registration papers to enter, but you will need to know your dog's full registered name and registration or R-number for filling out point forms should you win Winners or Reserve Winners competition.

POINT SYSTEM

The number of points awarded at any given show depends upon the number of dogs in competition.

Points	Dogs	Bitches
1	2	2
2	3	3
3	6	6
4	9	9
5	15	15

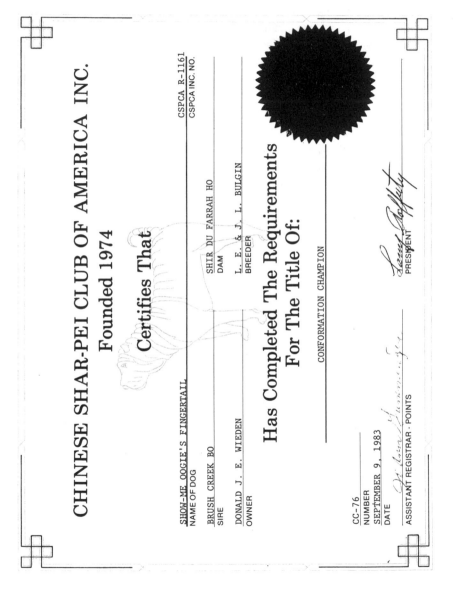

CHINESE SHAR-PEI CLUB OF AMERICA INC.
Founded 1974

Certifies That

SHOW-ME OOGIE'S FINGERTAIL
NAME OF DOG

CSPCA R-1161
CSPCA INC. NO.

BRUSH CREEK BO
SIRE

SHIR DU FARRAH HO
DAM

DONALD J. E. WIEDEN
OWNER

L. E. & J. L. BULGIN
BREEDER

Has Completed The Requirements
For The Title Of:

CONFORMATION CHAMPION

CC-76
NUMBER

SEPTEMBER 9, 1983
DATE

ASSISTANT REGISTRAR · POINTS

PRESIDENT

An example of a championship certificate issued by the Chinese Shar-Pei Club of America.

152

CHINESE SHAR PEI CLUB OF AMERICA, INC.

CONFORMATION/OBEDIENCE POINT SHEET

Owner_____ Phone #_____

Address_____

City_____ State_____ Zip_____

Name of Dog_____

CSPCA #_____ Whelped_____

Show_____ Date_____

Signature Show Chairman or Club Officer_____

Total Chinese Shar Pei in Competition Over Six (6) Months of Age:

Dogs: Class Entries_____ Champions_____

Bitches: Class Entries_____ Champions_____

Conformation Placement: WD WB BOW BOB GROUP 1 BIM / Points Applied For_____

Name Reserve Winners Dog_____ CSPCA #_____

Name Reserve Winners Bitch_____ CSPCA #_____

Best of Breed_____ Best of Winners_____ Best Opposite Sex_____

Obedience Class_____ Score_____

Name of Jr. Handler_____

Jr. Handler Class Entered_____ Placement ☐ 1 ☐ 2 ☐ 3 ☐ 4 Best Jr. Handler_____

Judges Signature (MUST BE LEGIBLE)_____

Applicant's Signature_____

I hereby certify that the above information is correct according to the records of this club.

Premium List, flyer or catalog *MUST* accompany point sheet to be valid.

You must be a member of the CSPCA for your dog to be eligible for points.

Each exhibitor is responsible for completing their own point sheet for each win.
Check with the CSPCA for current fees and the name of the point recorder.

The above list is the current Chinese Shar-Pei point system. It may change depending upon the percentage of major shows in a given year. Major shows carry point awards of three, four or five points. The American Kennel Club reviews its system throughout the United States annually. When a large percentage of shows have major entries, the number of dogs required in competition increases. Should the percentage of major shows fall below their guidelines, the numbers decrease. The CSPCA is responsible for the review and adjustment of Shar-Pei points.

When a dog accumulates a total of 15 points, which includes two major wins, he is deemed a champion. Once his championship is earned, the dog carries "Ch." before his registered name.

DAY OF THE SHOW

The best words of advice are: Come prepared. Most matches are held outdoors and in the summer. The clubs usually do not have tenting and shade is scarce. Many Chinese Shar-Pei don't tolerate heat well. Plenty of water, ice and a towel to wet the dog down are necessary supplies. Know your dog's limits. No show is worth losing your dog.

Matches are informal for the AKC-recognized breeds, but they are point shows for the rare breeds. Dress and act as if you were at an AKC-sanctioned point show. Rare breed people, including Chinese Shar-Pei fanciers, have worked long and hard to correct the "match show mentality" many judges possess. Everyone must realize that the rare breed handler is as serious and dedicated as any exhibitor at a point show.

Wear clothes that compliment your dog. The Chinese Shar-Pei is a color breed. When showing multiple dogs of different colors, select an outfit that will provide an effective backdrop for each dog. Do not wear clothing that overpowers or obscures the dog.

Always be polite and cooperate with the judge, stewards and fellow exhibitors. Unles complimentary, keep your remarks to yourself for the ride home. The Chinese Shar-Pei is a relatively new breed in the United States. The reputation of the breed depends on the behavior of the Shar-Pei fanciers. Once a reputation for unsportsmanlike behavior is established, it can take years to live it down.

Booklets containing all the show rules are available by writing the American Kennel Club, 51 Madison Avenue, New York, NY 10010 and the Chinese Shar-Pei Club of America, 55 Oak Court, Danville, CA 94526.

Junior handler Jennifer Kasoff winning Best Junior Handler in Match with Ch. Bruce Lee's Rumpole De Ruga.   *Bob Barber*

Ch. Peppermint Man Joss, owned by Kandi Stirling.

Ch. A-Capella's Pugs-Lee, owned by Curtis Phalen.

It may not be the Olympic gold,
but it's still 1st place.

PAPERWORK

The Chinese Shar-Pei owner is responsible for reporting all points earned. Each dog requires a separate form reporting all wins at any show.

Keep track of who takes Winners Dog, Reserve Winners Dog, Winners Bitch and Reserve Winners Bitch. You will need to ask the owner for his dog's registered name and R-number. Also, you will need to know the breakdown of the entry and the placements for Best of Breed, Best of Winners and Best of Opposite Sex.

Junior handling and obedience wins are reported on the same form.

To date, the CSPCA tallies junior handling scores on an annual basis. However, the club is not tracking Best of Breed, Group or Best in Show wins for specials. A special is a finished champion that is entered directly into the Best of Breed competition. The owner of the specials dog should keep meticulous records in order to prove outstanding wins when required. The *Kennel Review* Rare Breed of the Year Competition is by invitation only. The top dogs throughout the country compete. In order to select the Chinese Shar-Pei, the staff requires detailed resumes.

WHY SHOW THE CHINESE SHAR-PEI?

Aside from personal consideration, showing is an excellent way to promote a breed. Before the AKC will recognize a rare breed, there must be a history of activity throughout the United States.

In addition, your dog will be seen by many people at the shows. If you are planning to breed, shows are a good place to view potential stud dogs. Remember, however, that a championship title does not mean that the dog is the right one for your breeding program. Many people base their decision about breeding partners on titles and win records, and are often disappointed when the puppies are of lesser quality than the parents.

Shows are good experiences for the dogs. From the young puppy to the seasoned adult, dogs need to socialize with other dogs and people. A show dog is usually a trained, trustworthy dog that can handle himself in all types of situations.

Head type will become even more important as breeders try to resolve the Shar-Pei eye problems. Pictured are CSPCA Ch. Xanadu Genaul ISSI-Mo and CSPCA Ch. Genaul Megan Xanadu, CD owned by Helen Armacost. *Harkins*

12

Judging the Chinese Shar-Pei

$\mathbf{O}$NLY JUDGES LICENSED by the American Kennel Club may preside at sanctioned specialty shows. Currently, there are no restrictions on regular sanctioned events. Anyone may judge the Chinese Shar-Pei. The host club will select someone who they feel is qualified to judge the breed.

The Chinese Shar-Pei Club of America has voted to establish a system to approve non-AKC-licensed judges. Once finalized, this system will stipulate that judges will have to be AKC licensed or CSPCA approved.

MATCH VERSUS POINT SHOWS

Perhaps the biggest problem faced by Chinese Shar-Pei and other rare breed exhibitors is the "match show mentality" of many judges. They don't take the rare breeds seriously.

Chinese Shar-Pei shows are point shows, even though they are held in conjunction with match shows. A judge is determining the future of the breed by awarding points toward championship titles. Although the breeders and not the judges ultimately control the look of a breed, we all know that breeders tend to breed what the judges like. Many breeders look to championship titles and outstanding win records when considering a stud dog. It is up to the judges to make sure these champions are truly the best of the breed.

The "match show mentality" rears its ugly head in and out of the ring. Too few judges excuse or disqualify Chinese Shar-Pei. Few ribbons are withheld for lack of quality. While this may be acceptable at match shows, because they are just for fun, it is not acceptable at point shows.

Outside the ring, Chinese Shar-Pei judges are regularly approached before the show by exhibitors. Host clubs inviting Chinese Shar-Pei or any rare breed should set aside an area for the judges. Judges should not have to mingle with exhibitors for lunch or any other reason before their assignment.

Generally, what is unacceptable at an American Kennel Club point show is equally unacceptable at a Chinese Shar-Pei sanctioned event.

SPECIFIC POINTS FOR JUDGING SHAR-PEI

Once you determine that the dog under consideration has the requisite wrinkling that typifies the breed, forget the wrinkles. There is a dog under all that skin. Some judges, highly qualified in multiple breeds — even those similar in structure to the Shar-Pei — have done a questionable job with Shar-Pei because they couldn't get past the wrinkles.

The Shar-Pei should be an easy breed to judge. The coat is short, the musculature is well developed and little can be hidden from view. However, the Chinese Shar-Pei is deceptive. Many judges are able to predict from a first impression of the class at a dog show which dogs will be in the ribbons. First impressions of Shar-Pei can be misleading. Often the dogs that were impressive when stacked are poor in other areas and impossible to place.

The key to Shar-Pei is moderation. More is *not* better. The Shar-Pei is a medium-sized dog with a square profile. Your eye should travel from head to tail in one uninterrupted sweep. No one aspect of the dog should catch your eye. If it does, that element requires closer scrutiny.

The Shar-Pei is balanced. The large head is offset by the rise over the loin. When moving, the back will level out somewhat, but the characteristic "Trans-Am" rear will still be evident.

The movement of the Chinese Shar-Pei is powerful; there is good reach and drive. Rears are usually good. Problems are usually in the front assembly. Common problems include short forearms, bowing and lack of bend in the pasterns.

The Shar-Pei should move out at a vigorous trot. Too many dogs have been walked to their championships. As the judge, you may have to insist that the handlers move their dog out. Many Shar-Pei handlers are inexperienced. Willingness to instruct handlers in the ring is almost a prerequisite to judging Chinese Shar-Pei.

Ch. Noahs Ark Blackberry, CD.   *Bruce Harkins*

Will Chinese Shar-Pei prices go up or down? Only time will tell. Oriental Treasure's Xtra Trouble kissing Oriental Treasure's Tishen. Breeder: Maryann Smithers.

Ch. Gold's Rising Son.

While an experienced structure/movement judge can manage to put up a good Shar-Pei specimen, there are a few finer points that need to be understood immediately. The areas that most often cause problems include the ears, eyes, bite and tail sets.

The ears are small and held tightly to the head. If the ears attract your attention, they're probably too large. However, remember that the ears are highly mobile. A Shar-Pei can move his ears at will and in any direction. Be prepared to whistle or use a squeak toy to attract the dog's attention. When alert the ears will snap down into their proper position.

Be sure you check each dog's eyes. They should be dark and clear. Dogs that squint or have a tearing problem may have entropion. Any dog with eye problems should be excused. They belong in a veterinarian's office, not in the show ring.

Tails vary from nonexistent to long. Tails should be high set and carried over the back, falling to either side. They may be tightly curled, although the tip will still fall to either side. It is acceptable for the tail to be carried over, but not touching, the back.

Bites are hard to see. The padding of the muzzle makes parting the lips difficult. For health reasons, judges should ask the exhibitor to show the bite and mouth. Shar-Pei slobber. It is easy to transmit disease from one animal to another if the judge performs this procedure. However, judges should be aware that bad bites are common and be sure to fully inspect the mouth.

Coat is another area that has caused problems. Essentially there are two coats, horse and brush. The horse coat is very short, while the brush is slightly longer. No coat should exceed one inch in length at the withers. Be aware that the coat may appear longer than it actually is where wrinkling occurs.

Do not expect the Shar-Pei to animate in the ring. They are aloof with strangers. Some dogs get enthusiastic for bait or look adoringly at their owner. However, the deadhead should not be penalized for lack of animation. Even though the Chinese Shar-Pei is a head breed, it is the structure of the head not the animation that is important.

The standard for the Shar-Pei head is concise. The structure of the head stamps type onto each animal. Though very important, the head is not the whole dog. Placements because of head type only are not acceptable. The whole dog must be considered.

Finally, don't be afraid to consult the standard for the Chinese Shar-Pei. This is a relatively new breed in the United States and many judges have not had the opportunity to preside over Shar-Pei on a regular basis.

Even experienced judges may have to check a point or two. The standard is lengthy and you will see wide variations among some dogs. Exhibitors respect judges who take the time to do a conscientious job. However, never ask an exhibitor what is proper in the Shar-Pei, as you will certainly receive a wide range of answers.

Oriental Treasures Ugabee at four months. Owner: Maryann Smithers.

Crezentia

Ch. Lou-Ell's Topaz. *Bob Barber*

13

Working Chinese Shar-Pei

THE CHINESE SHAR-PEI love to please their owners and to work. Obedience training is relatively easy. Though highly intelligent, the breed matures slowly in mental and emotional capacities and may take longer to learn the commands.

Obedience training develops communication between the Shar-Pei and his owner. The Shar-Pei must respect his owner and this respect is earned. Obedience training helps put the pecking order in the proper perspective — you dog, me owner. A Shar-Pei will take command of his people and home if allowed.

Obedience training has several other benefits. Chinese Shar-Pei attract attention wherever they go. A well-trained dog is a good-will ambassador for the breed. Shar-Pei are still trying to live down the reputation of being a fighting dog. All contact with the public must be positive. In addition, obedience work helps relieve boredom and provides an outlet for the dog's accumulated energy.

Obedience titles are awarded by the Chinese Shar-Pei Club of America. CSPCA obedience titles are earned the same way as AKC titles. The only difference is that competitions are held at match shows where rare breeds are invited. Inform the obedience judge beforehand that you are competing for a leg toward a title. You will be in the ring with dogs who are there for practice only. Judges often allow corrections and tend to score more easily at match shows. He or she will be stricter with your entry.

A copy of the pamphlet outlining the obedience regulations is available at no charge from the American Kennel Club at 51 Madison Avenue, New York, NY 10010.

Preparing to stand for examination.
Danros Jolly Dragon, CD, at 14 weeks
at his first training session. Owned by
Rosie Lucitt.

Return to handler from the broad jump.
Lisa Norfolk

Return from the directed retrieve with
Rosie Lucitt.   *Lisa Norfolk*

The scent article exercise with wood and
metal articles.   *Lisa Norfolk*

Fritt's Han-Ho-Yan, CDX, retrieving over the high jump for judge Daniel J. Lucitt, Jr.

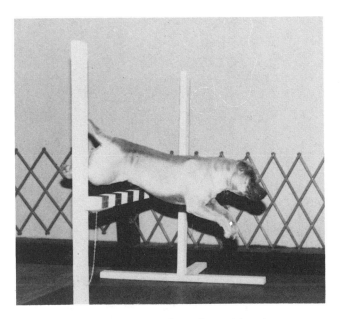

The utility bar jump from directed jumping.

Among Chinese Shar-Pei fanciers, the name Rosie Lucitt is synonomous with obedience. She owns the first CDX (Companion Dog Excellent) titled Shar-Pei in the United States. In 1986 she was awarded the Gaines Medal for Good Sportsmanship for work in the obedience field.

Rosie Lucitt's dogs also perform as therapy dogs. They visit hospitals, schools and nursing homes. The dogs take wheelchairs and walkers in stride, doling out kisses in return for smiles.

In order to become a therapy dog, a Shar-Pei must have exemplary social graces and be obedience trained. The dog must be certified by a reputable dog trainer as well as the owner. Dogs that qualify are registered with Therapy Dogs International. Therapy dogs work alone or in groups. It is expected that they will eventually be accorded the privileges given seeing eye or hearing ear dogs.

Another area where Shar-Pei have started to venture is Schutzhund training. The Schutzhund title originated in Germany and is becoming more popular in the United States. Tests include a combination of tracking, obedience and protection work. Good temperament is stressed. Shar-Pei should do well in advanced Schutzhund tests where the dog must make his own decisions.

The first Schutzhund titled Shar-Pei is Ling Chu's Mr. Magoo, owned by J. Sealy and Bobby Posa. Mr. Magoo received his DVG/Schutzhund title in 1984. This is a traffic obedience degree, involving basic obedience tests along with traffic security work. The security test is conducted in public areas with pedestrian traffic. The dog is expected to ignore strangers and remain quiet while the owner is out of sight. The dog is tried on and off lead. The DVG/Schutzhund title is recognized by the Chinese Shar-Pei Club of America.

Few Shar-Pei have earned obedience titles. This situation is due more to a lack of interest by owners rather than the Shar-Pei's ability. The Shar-Pei is a natural for obedience work and will perform well if given the opportunity. Currently the emphasis among Shar-Pei owners is on conformation competition rather than obedience trials.

Even without formal obedience training, the Chinese Shar-Pei leads a working life. The Shar-Pei is a dog with strong instincts for guarding, hunting and herding.

No one enters a Shar-Pei home without being announced. The Shar-Pei will alert his owner to the least disturbance in his environment. A sleeping Shar-Pei can become fully alert in an instant. Some dogs prefer to patrol the premises, looking for problems. Many dogs favor positions in front of a window. The Shar-Pei have eyesight equal to any sighthound

The Gung Ho Gang in the long sit.

The long down at Danros Kennels. Left to right: Fritt's Han-Ho-Yan, CDX, Jade of Hong Kong, CD and Danros U-Woof-O, CDX. The black lump to the right is Raven-dune Lyn-Del About Time, Am/Can. CDX.

170

and will spot prey or intruders long before the owner becomes aware of the disturbance.

The Shar-Pei hunter is patient. Sometimes compared to the cat, the Shar-Pei will wait for hours for the prey to surface. They are better mousers than are many cats.

Herding behavior can involve almost anyone. Puppies, children and even owners have experienced the desire of Shar-Pei to maintain togetherness.

Whatever purpose they serve, Chinese Shar-Pei make valuable additions to the household. They work, they love and they provide hours of entertainment.

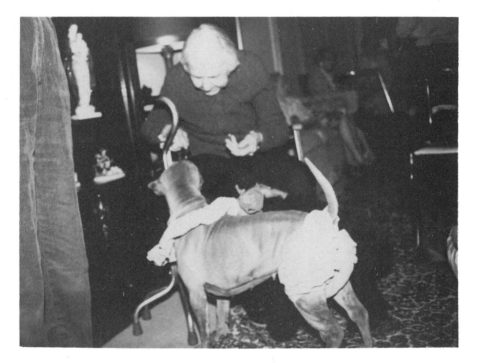

Danros U-Woof O, CDX, better known as Loosey, is a registered member with the Therapy Dogs International. Here she makes her rounds decked out in her favorite clown outfit. Owner: Rosie Lucitt.

Left to right: Ch. Bruce Lee's Wrinky Lee, Ch. Chow Wen Go Bamboo and Ch. Wow Wrinkette.

14

Chinese Shar-Pei
in the Media

EVERY CHINESE SHAR-PEI is a star. No Shar-Pei is immune from the attentions of his fans. Every walk down the street has multiple stops built in as other pedestrians stop to *ooh* and *aah* over his wrinkled face. Socialization is easy, but can be tough on owners and dogs in a hurry.

Some Shar-Pei have risen above the rest and made it in the commercial world. These dogs appear in newspapers and magazines across the country, visit national talk shows, pose for advertising photos and a few have even made it in the movies.

Today almost everywhere you turn, a Shar-Pei stares back. Their portraits appear on greeting cards, jigsaw puzzles, mugs and posters. America is fascinated by the Chinese Shar-Pei. The wrinkling provides line after line of humorous copy. The high purchase price gives them an air of aristocracy. The breed has become a status symbol in the commercial world. The Chinese Shar-Pei is big business.

The Shar-Pei that appear in most of these presentations were not selected for quality, although many are good examples of the breed. As with most dogs in the media, these were chosen for behavior, appearance or who the owner knows. Rarely is a talent search conducted for dogs. However, your chances are improved if your dog is obedience trained.

The Shar-Pei is an ideal public figure. Their aloof nature and attitude coupled with a calm disposition allow them to ignore all the disturbing activity taking place around them. Shar-Pei rarely exhibit fear. They pose

173

confidently as pictures are snapped and cameras roll. The born clown turns into a ham and loves every minute of his notoriety.

In the early years the Shar-Pei appeared in thousands of articles. The breed was rare and new to the United States. The dogs captured the imagination of the public. Everyone wanted to know about the most wrinkled and rarest dog in the world.

Leading the initial publicity blitz for the breed was Ernest Albright of Ho Wun Kennels. His Shar-Pei Gwei-Loh was the first dog listed in the *Guinness Book of World Records*. Fawn was pictured in over 600 newspapers and magazines and Ling Ling made the cover of *Dog Fancy* in 1977.

Two of Albright's Shar-Pei became movie stars. Shima debuted in a 1979 Japanese movie. Tara was selected to appear in the Disney movie, *The Billion Dollar Hobo*, with Tim Conway.

Albright's Shar-Pei, with or without their owner, have appeared in numerous television programs including "The Johnny Carson Show," "David Frost," "The Gary Moore Show," "To Tell the Truth" and "Good Morning America."

Albright's Fawn II achieved notoriety in a different area as the undefeated champion of Petaluma's Ugly Dog Contest.

The interest in Chinese Shar-Pei is still strong. Many owners who would never have dreamed of being in the public eye are suddenly doing photo sessions and making television appearances all because of their fascination with a Shar-Pei.

Valerie Fiorella's black Shar-Pei Kimo was recently selected to appear in the movie, *The Witches of Eastwick*, with Jack Nicholson. This was the highlight of Val's summer even though Kimo had to absorb a month's obedience training in three days and five minutes of film took all day to shoot.

Another veteran stage mother is Alice Lawler. She and her black Shar-Pei Rumpole appeared with animal expert Warren Eckstein on "The Saturday Morning Program" in New York. Struck by a slight case of stage fright, Alice answered the first three questions "Rumpole, Rumpole, Rumpole." On the same program, Alice's husband Jack turned out to be the natural television personality, even though he was handling the author's Peruvian Inca Orchid rather than one of their Shar-Pei.

Shar-Pei have also appeared on Canadian television. Gail Jordon's Doctor Love had his debut in conjunction with publicity for the annual Montreal Rare Breed Exposition sponsored by Jappy, a Canadian dog food company.

174

Print and television advertisers have all been eager to use the Shar-Pei. Many major department stores and manufacturers have featured the Shar-Pei in ads for almost any product, from oriental rugs to men's cologne. Macy's, Tilene's and Aramis are just a few of the more notable firms that have employed Shar-Pei.

Frisbee anyone? Owner: Helen Armacost.

Ch. Brush Creek Great Pumpkin. Owned by Madeleine and Pistol Tingen, A-Capella Kennels.

Ch. A-Capella Bojangles.

15

Affiliated Clubs

LOCAL DOG CLUBS are the sponsors of most of the major activities of the dog world. This applies to the Chinese Shar-Pei organizations as well as to those of any other breed.

Setting up any club is hard work. A constitution and by-laws must first be drafted and approved. It is always a good idea to legally incorporate so that the elected officers are not personally liable for any incidents that may occur. Officers must be selected. The club must apply for affiliation with the parent club before specialties can be sanctioned. The club needs a name, a logo, stationery. The start-up work is considerable.

Once formed, a number of activities are selected each year. Most clubs host one or more shows. Up to four shows may be sanctioned by any one club in a calendar year. The show itself takes a great deal of planning and effort. Working members are the lifeblood of any organization.

While the club benefits from its active membership, the membership derives benefits from belonging to the club. Owners meet other fanciers and exchange information. Programs are developed to educate the public and themselves. Members have an organized network for puppy and information referrals. Of course, everyone also has fun with their dogs at meetings and events.

The nature of the local club depends upon the officers and the personalities of the membership.

There are over 50 affiliated Chinese Shar-Pei clubs in the United States. More are being formed wherever multiple Shar-Pei and their owners reside.

The following are a few examples of active Chinese Shar-Pei clubs. Thanks go to Irene Campbell, Vivien Kelly, Debbie Houtz and Helen Armacost for supplying information on their local clubs.

THE MID-ATLANTIC CHINESE SHAR-PEI CLUB
Washington, D.C. area

In late 1981, Jo Ann Redditt and Arlene Richmond ran an advertisement in *The Washington Post* searching for people in the Washington, D.C., area who shared a love for the Chinese Shar-Pei breed and who were interested in the problems of obtaining and raising the rare breed dog. Sixteen people responded to this advertisement and on January 17, 1982 the first formal gathering of these fanciers was held in a private residence. In attendance were Bill, Scott and Gladys Arnold; Irene Campbell; Ronnie and Joyce Hanes; Ylva Lindgren; Madeleine and Michael Litz; Jill Parslow; Duncan and Jo Ann Redditt; Jud and Arlene Richmond and Ed and Barbara Sellers. The primary purpose of forming the club was mainly to devise a support system to deal with the purchasing of rare breed dogs and to cope with the various health problems. It also served as a wonderful social outlet and as an organization to put on dog shows.

The first officers nominated and elected to represent the club were: president, Jo Ann Redditt; vice president, Madeleine Litz; secretary, Irene Campbell; treasurer, Joyce Hanes; board members, Bill Arnold and Barbara Sellers. The Mid-Atlantic Chinese Shar-Pei Club was chosen as the official name.

The first year of the club was an ambitious one. The members wrote the constitution and by-laws, selected a logo, ran ads in the Washington area newspapers to obtain new members and established a monthly newsletter, with Jo Ann Redditt as editor, which contained news of the national club, new litter information, results of dog shows and general issues of interest to Chinese Shar-Pei dog owners. A brochure was printed with information on what the public needed to know before purchasing a Chinese Shar-Pei; handling classes were held for club members; speakers were invited to attend meetings — and all meetings ended with delightful buffet dinners.

On May 23, 1982, the members set up a Chinese Shar-Pei Fun Show held at the Litz farm in Clarksville, Maryland. Richard Tang was the judge. Because of the excellent publicity via radio and *The Washington Post*, hundreds of people turned out to see these wrinkled dogs and the Chinese Shar-Pei was on the way to becoming a very popular dog in the Washington area. Prior to the show, a handling class was held, and members brought food and items to be sold as a money-making project for the club.

On October 30, 1982, the Mid-Atlantic Chinese Shar-Pei Club sponsored its first specialty show. It was held at the fairgrounds in Timonium, Maryland. The judges were Ed Ray Sledzik and Paul Strang.

Ch. GK's Patrick of Bruce Lee. Owned by Bruce Lee and Tracy Resnick, Bruce Lee's Shar-Pei.

Ch. Pai-Gei's H.O.T. Stuff. Owned by Barbara and Gary Roche, House of Treasures.

Did someone say "horse coat!"

Ch. Krim Sun Red Hot Tamale.

Since the specialty show was in conjunction with the Baltimore rare breed clubs, it was a two-day show and members gained experience at dealing with hotel accommodations, publicity and the establishing of a hospitality room. The show attracted 51 entries.

The club hosted the national specialty show on July 1-3, 1984 at the Holiday Inn at Tysons Corner, Virginia. Each year the club also holds dog shows during the months of March and October.

The club has grown from an initial 16 members to 60 as of 1987. A Chinese Shar-Pei Rescue Unit has been established and the club also sponsors an autopsy fund so that fanciers might learn of the causes of death in the Chinese Shar-Pei. Donations are made to research projects such as the one now being conducted into the cause and treatment of megaesophagus in Chinese Shar-Pei.

SHAR-PEI CLUB OF THE NORTHEAST

The Chinese Shar-Pei Club of the Northeast was formed in September 1981 with a handful of people and has grown into 100 members who are well educated in many areas of the canine world. This is partially due to some of the programs the club has sponsored, which have included speaking engagements by veterinarians on a wide range of subjects, instruction on preparing your dog for the show ring by American Kennel Club judges, guidance by obedience professionals, discussions of homeopathic medicine and an all rare-breed slide presentation.

American Kennel Club judge Joan Urban and breeders of Shar-Pei gave us a better insight to the breed standard, while club member Linda Tintle, DVM, had the room overflowing with members. The club has also provided a seminar on the breed for American Kennel Club judges. Members were invited to the Gaines National Obedience Trials, where the dogs presented a very positive picture for the breed. The club had an information booth (complete with TV and VCR) at the AKC-sanctioned show held at the Meadowlands in New Jersey. This show is second only to Westminster in popularity and attendance. Thousands of packages of breed information were handed out that day.

The club newsletter is called the "News Wrinkle," with Linda Cejner as editor. It keeps the members informed on upcoming shows, events, brags, puppy announcements, national club news, "HIP" news, advertising, treasurer's report and health findings and contains a classified column. The club also maintains a library of assorted books.

The club held seven shows and brought in about $7,000 in revenues. The club has sent donations to many of the newer "sister" clubs to help

Ch. T-Time, a multiple Specialty
winner, owned by Joss Kennels.

Ch. E. F. Hutton. Owned
by Kandi Stirling, Joss
Kennels.

them put on their specialties and has always supported the national show either with trophies or a money donation.

The club honors members finishing dogs in conformation or obedience with a plaque at a year-end dinner.

GREATER TULSA SHAR-PEI CLUB

The Greater Tulsa Shar-Pei Club hosts two specialties a year (the first weekend in May and the second weekend in November). In addition, it usually teams up with the Green Country Rare Breed Club and the Sooner Aussie Club, making it a three-day show.

The club tried putting an ad in the local "Bargin Post," where the majority of ads appear for dogs for sale. It ran for six weeks in January and February and the club received 15 inquiries about Shar-Pei. Those people were sent a packet of information containing the national brochure, a copy of the standard, a membership form for the national club with the code of ethics, a membership form for our local club, order forms for the three Shar-Pei books out at that time and an order form for the *Orient Express II*. If they indicated interest in a puppy, a list of all club members with puppies or dogs for sale was enclosed. These people were then put on the show mailing list. The club intends to repeat this project several times a year.

The club members are currently planning a judges seminar, based on the one that was given in St. Louis, Missouri.

The list of officers for the Greater Tulsa Shar-Pei Club is: president, Debbi Houtz; vice president, Bonnie Berney; secretary, Patty Lucas; and treasurer, Helga Kamp.

CHINESE SHAR-PEI FANCIERS OF SOUTH FLORIDA

There are now two clubs and, hopefully, twice as many shows in the future for Shar-Pei fanciers. On May 1, 1986, the Chinese Shar-Pei Fanciers of South Florida, Inc. was established, and they quickly enacted a constitution, by-laws, a breeder's code of ethics and articles of incorporation.

The club has a membership of 32 Shar-Pei enthusiasts. At their first show, held on May 11, 1986 in association with the Boca Raton Dog Club (AKC), they posted 38 entries. Judge George Heitzman noted that he was very impressed with the overall entry and the club members' enthusiasm.

The club currently has two shows in the works and hopes to be able to

Ch. Bruce Lee's Keisha Deberic.

Gail Kernan

schedule future shows as much as six months to one year in advance so as to avoid conflicts with other clubs and AKC shows.

ARIZONA SHAR-PEI CLUB

The Arizona club boasts an increasing membership and an active show calendar. To help promote junior showmanship, the members of this club have agreed to lower their entry fees at the specialties and to include junior showmanship at their monthly matches. They also put on informative programs by noted speakers such as veterinary ophthalmologist Dr. Reuben E. Meredith, DVM.

The club makes annual donations to the Animal Benefit Club of Arizona, Inc., and to the National Humane Society. In addition, the club makes an annual contribution of books to the public libraries in their area to help educate the public regarding the Chinese Shar-Pei breed.

DELTA CHINESE SHAR-PEI CLUB

The Delta Chinese Shar-Pei Club is centered near the Mason-Dixon Line (Maryland and Pennsylvania). Delta received its parent club affiliation in May 1986.

The founding club officers were: president, Dennis Meredith; vice president, Kitty Shore; recording secretary, Helen Armacost; corresponding secretary, Jill Parslow; and treasurer, Heather Larsen.

The club is involved in many activities stressing fun, education and exposure for the breed in a positive light. The Delta Club decorated and sponsored a float in the large Bel Air, Maryland, July 4th Parade. Several members marched in the parade with the float, which received an Honorable Mention from the parade committee and rousing applause by onlookers the entire parade route for the regal array of wrinkled dogs in attendance.

The requirements for membership in the Delta Club are: filling out the membership form, a love of Chinese Shar-Pei, an open mind and a sense of humor.

Ch. Gung Ho's Eminent Domain. Owned by Peg Kastner, Eminent Kennels.

Bruce Harkins

16

The Chinese Shar-Pei and the Miscellaneous Class

NINETEEN EIGHTY-EIGHT may be the Chinese "Year of the Dragon," but it is the American "Year of the Chinese Shar-Pei."

The debate is finally over. After a long and controversial struggle, the Chinese Shar-Pei has been admitted to the American Kennel Club's Miscellaneous Class.

However, the struggle and the controversies are far from over. The breed still has a long way to go before being given full recognition by the American Kennel Club.

THE MISCELLANEOUS CLASS

The Miscellaneous Class constitutes the first official step toward AKC recognition for a rare breed. Much time and effort has preceded this moment and more of the same will follow.

Some people consider this class as a way station, while others call it a test period or holding pattern. No one knows how long the Shar-Pei will stay here. The breed could be moved along very quickly or it could remain in Miscellaneous for many years. It may never achieve full recognition.

Meanwhile, the AKC is viewing and reviewing the breed's activities throughout each year. Some of the items that are taken into consideration include:

1. The Chinese Shar-Pei Club of America as the sponsoring organization
2. The CSPCA registry and stud books
3. Demonstrations of substantial and sustained nationwide interest and involvement
4. Regular breed activities
5. Programs that promote and protect the breed in accordance with its standard
6. Resolution of any problems as identified by the AKC

THE INDEFINITE LISTING PRIVILEGE

As a member of the Miscellaneous Class, the Chinese Shar-Pei is eligible to be granted the Indefinite Listing Privilege on a dog by dog basis.

This ILP number allows you to enter your dog in Miscellaneous Class competition at licensed events, obedience trials and tracking tests. Your dog may compete for obedience and tracking titles, but not for points towards an AKC conformation championship.

In order to be issued an ILP number you are required to complete an application, submit pictures and pay the required fee. The AKC reviews the applications for acceptance and may request a meeting if there are any questions or problems.

Implicit in the designation, this registration is a privilege. The AKC reserves the right to deny assigning an ILP number and may cancel for cause at any time. In addition, litters of ILP registered dogs are not automatically eligible for ILP themselves. An application must be filed for each and every dog.

THE CHINESE SHAR-PEI CLUB OF AMERICA

The CSPCA is still the main managing body for the Shar-Pei in the United States.

According to AKC requirements, the parent club must continue to register dogs and maintain the stud books. It is through the parent club's sponsorship and activities that the AKC will evaluate the breed on the way to full recognition.

In addition, conformation titles are still the responsibility of the CSPCA. Undoubtedly, there will be some changes in the way shows are handled in the future. Some of these changes may include:

1. A method of awarding points for competition in the Miscellaneous Class
2. Greater restrictions on shows being sanctioned for points
3. Greater emphasis on specialty shows
4. Further restrictions on judge selection

Ch. Brush Creek A-
Capella Chang with
Madeleine Tingen

Ch. Aja's Gung Ho of Bucklee. Owned by Alice and Jack Lawler, Gung Ho Rare
Chinese Shar-Pei.   *Muller Studio*

189

Ch. Country Club's Whiz Bang I, owned by Elizabeth Hamilton-Hurley. *Harkins*

Ch. Country Club's Shur Two Bang, owned by Elizabeth Hamilton-Hurley *Kohler*

Technically, the Shar-Pei is still a rare breed. The rare breed shows will continue offering classes for the breed. Whether these classes will be matches or point shows depends on the parent club rules. The only real difference is that the Shar-Pei will be allowed to enter the Miscellaneous Class at sanctioned matches and licensed point shows.

CHAPTER 15, SECTION 9

This section of the Rules Applying to Registration and Dog Shows reads in part:

> A dog which is blind, deaf, castrated, spayed or which has been changed in appearance by artificial means except as specified in the standard for its breed . . . may not compete at any shows and will be disqualified . . .

This one rule is the greatest obstacle between the Chinese Shar-Pei and full AKC recognition.

From May 1988 on, no dog who has had his eyes tacked or entropion surgery may be shown in conformation competition. This rule would also apply to corrections for tight lip, stenotic nares and ear canal resections.

All these conditions and especially entropion affect the Shar-Pei's health. They are serious genetic problems that cannot be left to cure themselves. No show career is worth a dog's health or eyesight.

It is only through a concerted effort by responsible breeders that the problem will be solved. It will take time, but it can be done as proven by numerous other breeds in the past.

CLOSING COMMENTS

The future of the Chinese Shar-Pei is open to speculation. It's like watching the stock market — up or down. Only time will tell.

BIBLIOGRAPHY

ALL OWNERS of pure-bred dogs will benefit themselves and their dogs by enriching their knowledge of breeds and of canine care, training, breeding, psychology and other important aspects of dog management. The following list of books covers further reading recommended by judges, veterinarians, breeders, trainers and other authorities. Books may be obtained at the finer book stores and pet shops, or through Howell Book House Inc., publishers, New York.

BREED BOOKS

AFGHAN HOUND, Complete	Miller & Gilbert
AIREDALE, New Complete	Edwards
AKITA, Complete	Linderman & Funk
ALASKAN MALAMUTE, Complete	Riddle & Seeley
BASSET HOUND, New Complete	Braun
BLOODHOUND, Complete	Brey & Reed
BOXER, Complete	Denlinger
BRITTANY SPANIEL, Complete	Riddle
BULLDOG, New Complete	Hanes
BULL TERRIER, New Complete	Eberhard
CAIRN TERRIER, New Complete	Marvin
CHESAPEAKE BAY RETRIEVER, Complete	Cherry
CHIHUAHUA, Complete	Noted Authorities
COCKER SPANIEL, New	Kraeuchi
COLLIE, New	Official Publication of the Collie Club of America
DACHSHUND, The New	Meistrell
DALMATIAN, The	Treen
DOBERMAN PINSCHER, New	Walker
ENGLISH SETTER, New Complete	Tuck, Howell & Graef
ENGLISH SPRINGER SPANIEL, New	Goodall & Gasow
FOX TERRIER, New	Nedell
GERMAN SHEPHERD DOG, New Complete	Bennett
GERMAN SHORTHAIRED POINTER, New	Maxwell
GOLDEN RETRIEVER, New Complete	Fischer
GORDON SETTER, Complete	Look
GREAT DANE, New Complete	Noted Authorities
GREAT DANE, The—Dogdom's Apollo	Draper
GREAT PYRENEES, Complete	Strang & Giffin
IRISH SETTER, New Complete	Eldredge & Vanacore
IRISH WOLFHOUND, Complete	Starbuck
JACK RUSSELL TERRIER, Complete	Plummer
KEESHOND, New Complete	Cash
LABRADOR RETRIEVER, New Complete	Warwick
LHASA APSO, Complete	Herbel
MALTESE, Complete	Cutillo
MASTIFF, History and Management of the	Baxter & Hoffman
MINIATURE SCHNAUZER, New	Kiedrowski
NEWFOUNDLAND, New Complete	Chern
NORWEGIAN ELKHOUND, New Complete	Wallo
OLD ENGLISH SHEEPDOG, Complete	Mandeville
PEKINGESE, Quigley Book of	Quigley
PEMBROKE WELSH CORGI, Complete	Sargent & Harper
POODLE, New	Irick
POODLE CLIPPING AND GROOMING BOOK, Complete	Kalstone
PORTUGUESE WATER DOG, Complete	Braund & Miller
ROTTWEILER, Complete	Freeman
SAMOYED, New Complete	Ward
SCOTTISH TERRIER, New Complete	Marvin
SHETLAND SHEEPDOG, The New	Riddle
SHIH TZU, Joy of Owning	Seranne
SHIH TZU, The (English)	Dadds
SIBERIAN HUSKY, Complete	Demidoff
TERRIERS, The Book of All	Marvin
WEIMARANER, Guide to the	Burgoin
WEST HIGHLAND WHITE TERRIER, Complete	Marvin
WHIPPET, Complete	Pegram
YORKSHIRE TERRIER, Complete	Gordon & Bennett

BREEDING

ART OF BREEDING BETTER DOGS, New	Onstott
BREEDING YOUR OWN SHOW DOG	Seranne
HOW TO BREED DOGS	Whitney
HOW PUPPIES ARE BORN	Prine
INHERITANCE OF COAT COLOR IN DOGS	Little

CARE AND TRAINING

BEYOND BASIC DOG TRAINING	Bauman
COUNSELING DOG OWNERS, Evans Guide for	Evans
DOG OBEDIENCE, Complete Book of	Saunders
NOVICE, OPEN AND UTILITY COURSES	Saunders
DOG CARE AND TRAINING FOR BOYS AND GIRLS	Saunders
DOG NUTRITION, Collins Guide to	Collins
DOG TRAINING FOR KIDS	Benjamin
DOG TRAINING, Koehler Method of	Koehler
DOG TRAINING Made Easy	Tucker
GO FIND! Training Your Dog to Track	Davis
GROOMING DOGS FOR PROFIT	Gold
GUARD DOG TRAINING, Koehler Method of	Koehler
MOTHER KNOWS BEST—The Natural Way to Train Your Dog	Benjamin
OPEN OBEDIENCE FOR RING, HOME AND FIELD, Koehler Method of	Koehler
STONE GUIDE TO DOG GROOMING FOR ALL BREEDS	Stone
SUCCESSFUL DOG TRAINING, The Pearsall Guide to	Pearsall
TEACHING DOG OBEDIENCE CLASSES—Manual for Instructors	Volhard & Fisher
TOY DOGS, Kalstone Guide to Grooming All	Kalstone
TRAINING THE RETRIEVER	Kersley
TRAINING TRACKING DOGS, Koehler Method of	Koehler
TRAINING YOUR DOG—Step by Step Manual	Volhard & Fisher
TRAINING YOUR DOG TO WIN OBEDIENCE TITLES	Morsell
TRAIN YOUR OWN GUN DOG, How to	Goodall
UTILITY DOG TRAINING, Koehler Method of	Koehler
VETERINARY HANDBOOK, Dog Owner's Home	Carlson & Giffin

GENERAL

A DOG'S LIFE	Burton & Allaby
AMERICAN KENNEL CLUB 1884-1984—A Source Book	American Kennel Club
CANINE TERMINOLOGY	Spira
COMPLETE DOG BOOK, The	Official Publication of American Kennel Club
DOG IN ACTION, The	Lyon
DOG BEHAVIOR, New Knowledge of	Pfaffenberger
DOG JUDGE'S HANDBOOK	Tietjen
DOG PSYCHOLOGY	Whitney
DOGSTEPS, The New	Elliott
DOG TRICKS	Haggerty & Benjamin
EYES THAT LEAD—Story of Guide Dogs for the Blind	Tucker
FRIEND TO FRIEND—Dogs That Help Mankind	Schwartz
FROM RICHES TO BITCHES	Shattuck
HAPPY DOG/HAPPY OWNER	Siegal
IN STITCHES OVER BITCHES	Shattuck
JUNIOR SHOWMANSHIP HANDBOOK	Brown & Mason
OUR PUPPY'S BABY BOOK (blue or pink)	
SUCCESSFUL DOG SHOWING, Forsyth Guide to	Forsyth
WHY DOES YOUR DOG DO THAT?	Bergman
WILD DOGS in Life and Legend	Riddle
WORLD OF SLED DOGS, From Siberia to Sport Racing	Coppinger